# Historic Résumés
## of
# Famous Americans

by

Timothy B. Doe

*...and all history resolves itself very easily into the biography of a few stout and earnest persons.*

—RALPH WALDO EMERSON
Essays, *Self–Reliance* (1st Series, 1841)

General Publishing Group, Inc.
*Los Angeles*

*Publisher:* W. Quay Hays
*Editor:* Colby Allerton
*Art Director:* Maritta Tapanainen
*Production Director:* Nadeen Torio
*Projects Manager:* Trudihope Schlomowitz

*Photo credits for interiors and front cover:*
Library of Congress—P.T. Barnum, Samuel Clemens, Clarence Darrow, Stephen Foster, Anna Jarvis, Jack London, Billy Mitchell, Annie Oakley, Quanah Parker, Edgar Allen Poe, Queen Liliuokalani, Andrew Carnegie, Sitting Bull, Ambrose Bierce, J. Robert Oppenheimer, Tom Mix, Herman Melville, Marian Anderson, Susan B. Anthony, David Kalakaua, Pony Express, Henry Wells, William G. Fargo, Paul Robeson, Jack Johnson, Clara Barton;
Culver Pictures—Satchel Paige, Dorothy Parker, Gertrude Stein, James Thurber, Nikola Tesla, Jedediah Smith, George M. Cohan, Jim Thorpe;
Schomburg Center for Research in Black Culture: Billie Holiday, Marcus Garvey, Paul Robeson, Jackie Robinson, Josephine Baker, Harriet Tubman, Scott Joplin, Harry Houdini, Louis Armstrong, Will Rogers;
AP/Wide World—Amelia Earhart, Buffalo Bill Cody, Jay Gould;
Bettmann Archives—Wyatt Earp, Damon Runyon, Isadora Duncan;
Brown Brothers—Carry Nation, James Whistler;
Woody Guthrie Publications—Woody Guthrie;
Arizona Historical Society/Tucson #17345—Geronimo;
Grace College—Billy Sunday;
Paramount Productions, 1936—Francis Farmer;
Sierra Club—John Muir;
Courtesy of Levi Strauss & Company—Levi Strauss;
By Permission of Houghton Library, Harvard Library—Emily Dickinson;
Pancho Zuckerman Collection—B. Traven;
Courtesy of Kentucky Fried Chicken Corporation—Harland Sanders;
Courtesy of Bart Doe—Emmett Kelly;
Courtesy of International Church of the Foursquare Gospel—Aimee Semple McPherson;
Copyright 1928 by Herbert G. Ponting—Charlie Chaplin;
Archives of Labor and Urban Affairs, Wayne State University—Joe Hill;
Courtesy of Girl Scouts of the U.S.A.—Juliette Gordon Low;
Charles L. Webster & Company, 1887—George Custer;
Courtesy of Arnold, Schwinn & Company—Ignaz Schwinn.

For information:
General Publishing Group
2701 Ocean Park Boulevard, Suite 140
Santa Monica, CA 90405

Printed in the USA
10 9 8 7 6 5 4 3 2 1

General Publishing Group
Los Angeles

# Introduction

A long time ago, when the world seemed young, eager, and optimistic, I adopted the ostensible profession of travelling the country while pursuing various occupations and employments, or, as those concepts are sometimes referred to, work. As stated, this was a long time ago. My present career, if such it can be called without mocking the millions of people who take the concept seriously (and for whom, regardless of how I conduct the mad exercise in folly which is my life, I have the greatest respect) is of a somewhat unusual nature, in that I don't function within the generally accepted linear restraints of time, space, motion, and respectability. This has often caused me to wonder if there isn't an Indian lurking somewhere in the ancestral woodpile. At any rate, fate has chosen to provide me the necessities of survival in this wild world while remaining within the bounds of the law and common decency, and for this I am, and shall always be, eternally grateful.

But I'm sure that's enough said about that. My purpose here is to provide a brief and succinct explanation as to how these documents came to be discovered, then to gratefully retire to my habitual obscurity—so in order to do so I must move along.

I had put in at Morgan City, Louisiana in April of the year, having crewed aboard a 125 foot fishing boat down from the Aleutian Islands. This was a good job, as far as that goes, as it paid a comfortable daily wage and required little more than standing wheel watches and painting. I had worked on deck during the previous crab season, which time the boat's owners saw the folly of attempting to fish the Bering Sea in a vessel designed for the Gulf of Mexico. To clarify this, if it is your intention to go to sea in that region during the season of active weather (which in those latitudes can be considered 12 months a year), you should do so in a boat that draws some water, not a shallow draft oil rig tender from Louisiana. Real Bering Sea boats come out of the Puget Sound yards, anyway. So I left the *Virgo* tied up at the docks on Six Mile Lake, collected my pay, and took the bus to New Orleans where, for eight hundred dollars, I bought a twenty year old Chevrolet pick up truck with a camper on it from a Petty Officer who was mustering out of the Naval Station at Algiers. It seemed solid and road worthy, brakes were good, tires were fair, so I equipped it with necessary gear from a surplus store and a week's worth of groceries and headed north out of town in a late afternoon thunderstorm. Destination? New York City.

Noon of the third day out of New Orleans found me on the eastbound approaches to the Holland Tunnel out of Jersey City with vague designs of ending up in Brooklyn. I let the traffic carry me along Canal Street toward the Manhattan Bridge, then turned south, however, for I felt it would prove to be better *feng shui* to cross over the Brooklyn Bridge. This was, after all, my first visit to Gotham. I took the first exit off the bridge, crossed Cadman Plaza onto Middagh, and came up to the stop light at Hicks. And there, dead center in the middle of the intersection, the transmission detached itself from the truck and fell to the pavement, bursting apart like an overripe watermelon dropped from a stepladder. I was marooned for fair. It was a marvel to see how fast the money went during the next four hours. Only in retrospect, of course—at the time it seemed serious. There was a ticket for obstructing traffic, the tow charges, an outlandish fee for a secure storage yard for the truck, a deposit paid to a mechanic toward the purchase of a new transmission, and finally, as to live in the camper was impossible while it remained in the fenced storage facility, a week's rent in a faded hotel off the Bowery on the Lower East Side, secured on the recommendation of a cabbie. So began my time in Brooklyn Heights, an appropriate setting for the literary adventure that was to follow.

Naturally, the mechanic discovered something rare and unusual about the transmission and found it impossible to locate a replacement in the 'cuppla days' he had promised. Time went on, all the while my financial status becoming less and less enviable. I was no stranger to work (as I've stated), being much younger then, so it looked like it was time to go out and try to find some. This need was solved in the time-honored tradition when, while pondering over the situation in a neighborhood tavern, I met a chap named Earl Hadley Hurlbut, Jr., a building contractor specializing in the refurbishment of older structures which, as older is the rule rather than the exception in Brooklyn, stayed as busy as he chose on the strength of an admirable local reputation nurtured by his exuberant and effusive happy-glad-hander style, a single-minded attitude toward work, and his traditional methods of doing business. Suffice it to say that these methods had their foundation in his habit of carrying large amounts of cash around and, utilizing his uncanny instinct of knowing when the time was right, being as free with it as the situation warranted. He summed up his philosophy along these lines one time, and I'll never forget it: "There's no pockets in burial shrouds, laddie." I liked Earl.

So I went to work, which happy fact led to my spending a lot of time in Brooklyn Heights in the ensuing months. I want to make it clear that by no means should that be construed to mean I truly got to know the place, for I am of the opinion an entire lifetime is required to make that claim. However, as history has always been my passion, and I did play at least a nominal role in the discovery of these documents, I feel I am entitled to state, without appearing pretentious, my belief that the significance of Brooklyn Heights as the setting of this tale is of the utmost merit, in that this particular *arrondissement* of the great metropolis is possessed of a historical literary pedigree that is preeminent within the full scope of the American experience.

As an employee of the Hurlbut Renovation & Restoration Company (generously underwritten by Earl's father, Earl Hadley Hurlbut Sr., an opinionated octogenarian who had made his money in dirigibles during the heyday of that marvelous technology), my first assignment was to begin organizing the remodeling of a two story structure on Cranberry near Cadman Plaza, reputedly very near the location of the print shop where Walt Whitman typeset the first editions of *Leaves of Grass*. I made the mistake of mentioning this tidbit to Earl, who responded in the fashion I would soon learn to consider characteristic: "So what. Let's get something done."

This contract was completed on schedule and under budget and, being duly given some credit for this accomplishment, I was assigned to supervise the subsequent, somewhat more ambitious, project. Involved here was the renovation of a three and a half story brick building on the southeast corner of Middagh and Hicks, the very corner, you'll recall, that had claimed the transmission. The structure was a classic example of the early 19th century designation of '1st Class Brick Store,' thirty feet wide and fifty deep, dating probably to the days of Andy Jackson's administration. There were two ground floor entries on the Hicks Street side, one at the center, and one leading to the upper floors at far right. Large whitewashed plate glass windows flanked the center doors, and each of the upper three floors featured a row of four windows. The fire escapes were front center, and stone entablature topped off the west and north sides.

Something fortuitous happened now, although I couldn't know it at the time. It turned out that Earl's presence was required at his development in central Florida, where he was attempting to transform a couple of hundred acres of malarial and pestilent swampland into a retirement paradise. He was going to be gone for a couple of weeks, so he gave me the keys to the building, a set of blueprints, and these instructions:

"Now, listen, laddie, I wancha to get the ground floor cleared out and cleaned up. It's a mess, on account of nobody ain't been in there since Julius Caesar was President. Throw away all the trash, but take care of them desks and cabinets, on account of Solly Rubinstein's gonna pay me good money for 'em, on account of they're antiques. Frame up what I got drawn on the prints, and knock out the sections of the walls that I got marked in red, don't worry, they ain't bearing walls, and cart out all the rubbish. The lumber delivery is comin' a week from tomorrow, so have it clean by then. Hire a couple stew bums to cart it inside, and make sure they stack it up neat. Do this right, and I'll getcha a new chalkline…." And so on.

A cold rain fell as I walked from the Jay Street subway station, arriving a little after seven a.m. The key turned the front door lock with an ease unexpected from such an old mechanism, and I let myself in on the ground floor. I don't feel it is necessary to go into a great amount of detail regarding the specifics of the entire floor, so suffice it to say it consisted of a reception area fully as wide as the building and about twenty feet deep, three offices containing a number of examples of antique utilitarian office furniture, and a hallway extending from the back of the reception room to the back of the building. The offices were accessed from doors in the reception area and the hallway, two on the left of the hall and one to the right. I spent the first day studying the layout of the building, exploring the individual rooms, and going over the prints. Everything seemed fairly straightforward and common, but that was hardly to be the case.

It wasn't until the next morning that I first became aware of the discrepancies in the blueprints. Earl had indicated which walls he wanted worked on, and one of those was the back wall of the solitary office which opened into the right side of the hallway. This wall was constructed of red brick and, according to the prints, I was to frame up a section of 2x4's directly onto it and prepare it for plastering. It was while going in and out of the door to this office that I noticed something. Looking down the hall toward the back of the building I could see the two entrances to the left side offices, but why weren't there any more doors on the right side? I re-examined the prints. The back wall of the office I was working in and the right wall of the hall formed a right angle creating an area of approximately 800 square feet which was, most curiously indeed, inaccessible from any point on the ground floor. I examined the outside of the building and confirmed my suspicions: it was completely sealed off. This was remarkable. I returned to the office for a closer examination and discovered that there was an area at the center of the wall, roughly the shape of a door, where the brick and grout were of a slightly different texture and color than that of the wall itself. Although it was not part of my assignment, I could not contain my curiosity and, fetching a 24 ounce framing hammer and cold chisel, I began to remove the bricks from the ancient entry. After a couple of hours I had created an opening the size of the original door and, dragging along a drop light on the end of a long cord, I entered the mysterious sanctum which would prove to be the long forgotten offices of Pietro's Placement Service.

The air in the room was dead, and permeated with tangible, clutching qualities of antiquity and decay. An extremely fine dust covered everything, and was of such a delicate nature that my slightest movement caused small clouds to rise. With the exception of a three piece gilt framed mirror hanging between the two bricked in windows, the unpretentious plastered walls and simple oak panel wainscot were unadorned. The room itself was, in essence, the same as the others on the floor and possessed no singularly distinctive or noteworthy characteristics. Excepting, of course, the furnishings. Three quarters of the floor space was occupied by an array of perfectly preserved, collection-quality antique furniture arranged in a fashion to suggest storage rather than function, with room to walk between. There were, in no particular order, two identical mahogany block-front desks and matching kneehole commode, a long-case clock with the case veneered in walnut and enriched with chased and gilded brass, several marble top side tables, a matching pair of oak draw tables with ornately carved legs and inlaid frieze, two Empire consoles, a small writing table of the Sheraton period which boasted an ingenious arrangement of drawers and sliding top, four matching walnut lowboys, two Chippendale mahogany ladder-back side chairs, four (three right-hand, one left) hickory, maple, and walnut windsor writing armchairs, a ten-legged bamboo-turned windsor wooden settee with spindle-filled back & ends, two tall mahogany whatnots with canterbury, a Duncan Phyfe mahogany drop-leaf table, a number of matching oil lamps with triple-flute pattern fonts on marble bases and, standing dominant over this most impressive collection, two magnificent mahogany breakfront bookcases six feet tall and nearly as wide. I was astounded. Earl had mentioned taking care of the desks and cabinets that were in this building but there was no way he could have known of the existence of the pieces in this sealed room. Granted, the furniture in the other offices undoubtedly had value as antiques or, at the very least, collectibles, but nowhere near the worth of these museum quality specimens. Making a conscious effort to control my excitement, I began my investigations, completely forgetting about the work I was supposed to do.

In addition to the furniture, there were dozens of plain oak storage crates, 14 inches wide, 26 long, 10 deep, carefully packed with an enormous variety of papers, forms, stationery, letterhead, brochures, bundles of mail, vouchers, invoices, clippings, journals, folios, logs, day books, pamphlets, and assorted ephemera; three mint condition antique typewriters, two of which were Remington (Standard Typewriter No. 2 and a Noiseless) and a World War I era Royal Standard; a baffling array of office supplies—pens and quills and inkwells and clips and postage stamps and French curves and blotters and organizers and drafting tools and stenographer's supplies and God only knows what else; a dictaphone machine; reams of parchment, kraft, vellum and onionskin; reference books, dictionaries, thesauri, directories, style guides, almanacs, and a complete set of the Revised Series of McGuffey's Readers in original condition. Amongst the McGuffey's I made a rather singular discovery—a little book, ancient and brittle, slightly over six by four inches in size, stitched, without wrappers, entitled *Tamerlane and Other Poems*, by A Bostonian. It carried the printer's ornament Boston, Calvin F.S. Thomas, Printer, 1827.

My explorations began in earnest. I carefully went through one of the crates, then another, and another. In the third I discovered an 9x12 cardboard box containing a couple hundred sheets of yellowed watermarked bond imprinted with an ornate 19th century letterhead embellished with archaic typeface and elaborate calligraphic flourishes. The letterhead read "Pietro's Placement Service—Luminiferous Tomorrows Begin With Diligent To-Days." Why, it was an old employment office, or something very much like it. Next was a crate containing carefully indexed invoices, bills, and statements arranged chronologically and dating back to…what's this? 1831? Incredible! Four crates held the invoicing materials, and it became apparent that every year from 1831 to the mid-1960's was represented. I stayed in there until eleven o'clock that night, stopping only once to eat until, thoroughly exhausted, I locked up and caught a late train, dizzy with the magnitude of my discovery.

I was back at dawn and turned my attention to the two bookcases, each of which were divided into two sections, the top two thirds containing three shelves protected by four framed doors set with beveled glass. Ornately inlaid solid mahogany doors covered the four cabinets below. Each of these pieces contained about fifteen hundred file folders constructed of heavy 12x17 foolscap, folded widthwise and labeled with a small paper flag bearing a name. These were carefully stored and arranged alphabetically by surname. I took one down from the left side of a top shelf and opened it. It contained sheets of handwritten notes, a carbon copy of an invoice, and various typewritten and corrected drafts of what appeared to be a brief personal and occupational synopsis of an individual. I replaced it and inspected a couple dozen more, and soon discovered the theme. These documents were apparently produced by Pietro's Placement Service as a means of assisting their clients to obtain employment or other goals and objectives. I saw materials produced for a wheelwright, a harbor pilot, a seamstress, a lamplighter, a schoolmarm, a cantor, a cooper, a circus acrobat, and a painless dentist. The person's professional experience was described in detail, and certain other attributes were factored in on what seemed to be an individualized, as-needed basis. Well-written, concise, and thorough, I gathered through certain evidence that they were produced by different writers over a long period of time, and yet bore certain similarities of diction and phrasing, as if written by various students of the same mentor. Fascinated, I moved through the stacks until I came to the letter 'C', and there made the first of the many historically significant discoveries as I retrieved a file, identical in every respect to all the others, labeled 'Custer, Geo. A.'

I stood there staring at it for the longest time, saying over and over "this can't be, this can't be". But it was. According to this evidence, General George Armstrong Custer had, in January of 1876, paid Pietro's Placement Service eight dollars and fifty cents to produce a chronicle of his professional background, or résumé, if you will, in order to persuade the War Department to send him out in command of an expedition to tackle the Sioux in the Western Wilderness. I wouldn't mind, at this point, stating that I feel I am in the position to take a little credit concerning my awareness of the enormous significance of what I had uncovered, as well as revealing the gratitude I felt knowing that I would be left alone with the discovery for the next ten or so days. So I didn't waste any time establishing a schedule, to which I adhered with religious determination.

Five hours of the day were given over to completing as much construction work as would be expected in eight while ten were spent either with the résumés or conducting library research. This left nine hours to eat, commute, and sleep. I inspected each and every one of the approximately twenty-eight hundred files, and soon developed an eye for what I was after, which helped speed up the process. I purchased a comprehensive biographical dictionary at the used bookstore and developed an effective little system of cross-referencing as I made further discoveries. The end result, after about ninety hours of intensive work, was the production of a hand-written master list containing the names of a large number of historically significant persons representing a wide and diverse panorama of nearly fourteen decades of American history. It became apparent that Pietro's Placement Service had been operated through the years by succeeding generations of the family and had established a solid professional reputation and an enviable referral customer base which insured the longevity and prosperity of the enterprise over a very long period of time. In addition, the evidence indicated that the operational philosophy of the service was one of strict confidentiality and that although so many of their clients were renowned to varying degrees, and became more so as the years went by, never was it the intent of Pietro's to publicize or capitalize on the rather unique and intimate relationships they developed with the individuals to whom they provided their services. I would like to mention here that I personally have a great respect for a business philosophy of this nature, so rare in these modern times, and that I have on occasion questioned the propriety of presenting these documents to the public even at this late date. I have become convinced, however, that the historical importance of Pietro's legacy justifies the present publication, and will in no way prove harmful or compromising to the memories of the individuals profiled. As regards other pertinent aspects of the business, I continued to uncover information. Six of the crates were labeled 'Kansas City/San Francisco,' and my detective work revealed that, at the height of their prosperity, Pietro's established branch offices at these locations. Invoices, statements, and other materials gave the dates of the operation of these locations as 1861-1920 and 1873-1939 respectively, and records showed that all the files from these branches were shipped to New York upon the closing of the office. In addition, postal receipts revealed that a certain percentage of work was conducted by correspondence— which explains the European addresses, for example. Another noteworthy point is the indications that the service, in the autumn of its dynasty, developed an especially active following within the worlds of theatre, art, music, and the cinema. For instance, there were quite a number of future famous rock'n'roll musicians who secured Pietro's services in the 1950's and '60's, and who—but I must take care not to digress from the central purpose of this introduction. At this juncture I would like to bring up one important point that I have not, to this day, been able to resolve: What became of Pietro's Placement Service? Who were they? For months and even years afterwards I searched all sources, tracked and traced, dug through endless business directories, land conveyances, title records, and telephone books, even hired professional help, but was never able to locate even one person who could shed some light on the fate of any of the Pietros. There must be an answer somewhere, and I doubt I'll ever quit trying to find it.

Earl returned from Florida a day late, and left a message at my hotel to meet him at the building the next morning. He and I conducted a brief walk-through of the ground floor, and it didn't take him long to spot the wall that I'd opened up.

"What's goin' on? Whaddaya knockin' holes in the wall…."

I turned on the drop light. "You better take a look at this, Earl."

Thus began a long and involved period of activity centered around Earl's position as the licensed contractor and the rights of the owner of the building, an elderly gentleman farmer from upstate named Ralph Fielding Snell. Turned out that the furniture was quite valuable—*quite* valuable—and that fact became the complete and total obsession of these two gents, to the exclusion of the renovation and everything else. Earl had learned years ago of the distinct possibility of this kind of thing happening, especially in an antiquated locale like Brooklyn Heights, and had slipped into his contract the tiniest clause regarding discoveries of this nature and his legal claim to them. Earl's response to Ralph's protest that he hadn't seen that particular clause was memorable and very amusing. As you might well imagine, they went at it tooth and nail, all the while dealing with appraisers, collectors, lawyers, antique dealers, etc. This gave me the opportunity to maintain a low profile, and I waited until I sensed the time was right to bring up the subject of the file folders in the bookcases. They were discussing shipping the furniture out to a more secure storage facility when I interrupted them.

"I was wondering about all those files that are in the bookcases. What are you going to…do with those?"

Snell regarded me impatiently. "Those folders? I don't know. What's in them?"

"Well," I replied, "this was an old employment office, as you know, and apparently those documents are applications, profiles, that kind of thing. They're histories of the clients that came to this service…."

"Let me see."

He went over to one of the bookcases, selected a file at random, and gave it a cursory inspection.

"So. This is something written for a guy who was a timekeeper at the navy yard—he worked there a long time after the First World War…interesting." He paused as I held my breath, and I held it until I saw his eyes light up with his decision. "But this isn't worth anything. You want them, Earl?"

"Those? What, old job applications? Get rid of 'em."

I managed to act disinterested.

"How about if I just pack them out of here and store them somewhere? Maybe later they...."

Earl gave the slightest wave of his hand. "Take 'em to the dump, do whatever, I got things to do."

So, happy as an angel half full of pie, I located a wholesale stationery supply and purchased three dozen cheap plastic storage crates and had each and every file packed away by the end of the day. I enlisted the help of a perceptive and astute librarian I had met at one of the branches and, borrowing Earl's truck, we cached them away in the basement of the library where she worked in Manhattan and where they remained, safe and sound, for nearly two decades.

So ends the saga of the discovery of the résumés. I would like to mention, however, that Earl and Ralph weren't exactly stupid when it came to recognizing the worth of other items that were uncovered. The ornately engraved .30-.30 Winchester with the inscription "To G. Pietro, thank you for everything, Buffalo Bill Cody," or the small magician's prop box with Harry Houdini's New York address stenciled on the lid, or one of Louis Armstrong's mouthpieces with his initials on it, or the the Bowie knife with "Geronimo" painted on the sheath—they didn't miss that stuff, although they never did connect the famous names with what the files might contain. I showed Snell the little book I'd found with the McGuffey's Readers. He looked at it, stated his opinion that it couldn't have much value if it didn't even have an author's name on it, and, after the fashion of a person throwing a dog a bone, made a magnanimous showing of giving it to me. As Ralph is no longer of this world, I don't feel he will be hurt by my disclosing the identity of the volume. It is, if you didn't know, the first collection of Edgar Allan Poe's poetry ever printed, of which previously only four had been known to exist.

Why did I wait nearly twenty years to publish these remarkable documents? Well, for one thing, I went out into the world and did a thousand things, travelled to a thousand places and met ten thousand people. I learned a lot and became, I believe, a better person for it. But there's another reason, and it has to do with the approaching end of the millennium. I am of the belief that we are poised on the brink of a vital and spirited new era, a time when the coming generations will not focus their life energies solely on the acquisition of wealth and material goods, a time when the universities won't be glutted with freshmen whose only long range plans are corporation lawyer or MBA, a time of true elegance and style which will provide a fertile nurturing ground for generations of productive, original, inspired, and visionary people who will not have to apply a disproportionate amount of their creative drive towards simple survival while enjoying a true measure of acceptance, respect, and recognition of worth from the status quo. This has led me to the conviction that now is an appropriate time to present the brief biographies of the 70 (Wells & Fargo count as two) significant Americans you are (hopefully) about to peruse, and to do my small part to promote the sense of place and being that stems from achieving a solid understanding of history. For when better than now, so near the end of the Twentieth Century, to contemplate the lives, achievements, and contributions of those who have gone before, and to come to understand the lasting legacy and overall impact of the great American experiment that, for all its flaws, will remain the most uninhibited, diverse, influential, confident, and vigorous social adventure the world will ever know. And, by Jings, if that's not an optimistic outlook I certainly would like to know what is.

# Acknowledgments

Dedicated to Thomas Berger, because without *Little Big Man* this never would have happened.

To do a proper job with these acknowledgements it is of course imperative to begin with the countless public libraries in the twenty or so Western states (as well as a few back East) I visited while doing the biographical research. A comprehensive listing of these libraries isn't really practical, for a variety of reasons that I'd rather not get into here, but I would like to acknowledge a few that stand out in memory. The literary detective work began with the Multnomah County (Oregon) Public Library and concluded with the Los Angeles, California system, two fine organizations. In between I recall libraries in San Diego, Oakland, Marysville, Palm Springs, Placerville, Burbank (especially Burbank), Glendale, Pasadena, and Kings Beach, California; the UCLA Special Collections Library; Hilo, Hawaii; Tombstone, Bagdad, Globe, Safford, and Casa Grande, Arizona; Ketchum, Hailey, Coeur d'Alene, and Orofino, Idaho; Bandon and Hood River, Oregon; Laramie, Wyoming; the Zimmerman Library at the University of New Mexico, Albuquerque; Deming, New Mexico; Plano, Lubbock, Sweetwater, and Dallas, Texas; Chicago, Quincy, and Highwood, Illinois; Lawrence, Council Grove, and Leavenworth, Kansas; Hannibal, Missouri; Hardin, Montana; Sterling, Durango, and Cortez, Colorado; Alma and Friend, Nebraska; Reno, Carson City, and Incline Village, Nevada; Vancouver, Seattle, and Bellingham, Washington; Denver, Iowa; Delevan and Oshkosh, Wisconsin; Big Rapids and Monroe, Michigan; the New York Public Library and a whole host of others. I would like to express my deepest gratitude to these institutions and the dedicated individuals who staff them, none of whom will have the slightest idea who I am.

———— ◆ ————

It is quite impossible to thank Vincent Bugliosi enough, for it moved into high gear that fateful winter's day in the résumé office when he found Mike Hamilburg's (literary agent *extraordinaire*) number on the scrap of paper in his wallet and suggested I call.

I doubt William Kennedy and Evan Connell remember my correspondences, but their gracious responses to my naive and eager fan letters were true and pronounced sources of inspiration, and sincerely appreciated.

Thanks are in order to Emmy Cresciman, accomplished résumé writer as well as my reliable sounding board; Gene Estrada, Senior Librarian with the Los Angeles Public Library, a truly competent professional; Bob Baxter, of CareerPro Résumé in Glendale, for his patient tolerance and understanding; Marla Conti, enthusiastic and capable Senior Researcher, and her able assistants Annie (my daughter) and Rachel (my goddaughter); Joanie Socola of the Mitchell J. Hamilburg Agency, for helping me get through some stormy weather; Ed Conti, for letting me park that beat up little pickup truck in the driveway for so long; Robert "Red" Johnson, owner of the Culpepper & Merriweather Circus, for giving me the opportunity to be a 24 Hour Man; Theresa O'Neill-Johnson; Bob Kellogg, circus historian; John Ortiz, creative consultant; Rob Healy; Linda Troxell; Phil Harvey; my sister Jenni; Joy King; my Dad—Bart Doe—and Mary, for their ongoing help and support; Gloria R. Estrada, for tolerating my hobo ways; and finally, my brother Dave for believing in it from the start. Residents of Brooklyn Heights and other astute readers will recognize the building on the corner of Middagh and Hicks as the current home of the Court Street Coffee Bar, owned and ably operated by Paula and Ezi Gibly, to whom I am indebted for their cooperation.

Professional assistance was provided by Diane Hamilton, photographic researcher of Washington, D.C.; The Library of Congress; Brown Brothers Photographic Archives, Sterling, Pennsylvania; Debbie Goodsite and Jennifer Marshall, Bettman Archives, New York; Tim Feleppa, Culver Pictures, New York; Colby Allerton, General Publishing Group; The Arizona Historical Society, Tucson; Robert McCracken, Paramount Pictures Studio Archives, Los Angeles; Joe Coomber, photographer; Mary Samples, Angelus Temple, Los Angeles; The Colby Library of the Sierra Club, San Francisco; Jean Litterst, Director of Public Affairs, Kentucky Fried Chicken Corporation, Louisville, Kentucky; The Tom Mix Museum, Dewey, Oklahoma; Walter P. Reuther Library of Labor and Urban Affairs, Wayne State University, Detroit; Houghton Library, Harvard University; Grace College, Winona Lake, Indiana; Mary Levey, Director, National Historic Preservation Center, Girl Scouts of the U.S.A.; Levi Strauss & Company, San Francisco; Industrial Workers of the World, Chicago & Los Angeles; Alan Taylor Communications, New York; The Brooklyn Historical Society; Schomburg Center for Research in Black Culture, New York Public Library.

# Table of Contents

At the conclusion of a concert on one of her earlier European tours, she was taken aback when the audience failed to applaud. It wasn't what she thought, though—they were simply too astounded to respond. The incident that made her famous in this country occurred when the Daughters of the American Revolution refused to allow her to perform in Constitution Hall in Washington (Eleanor Roosevelt resigned her membership in protest), and the concert that followed, attended by 75,000 people at the Lincoln Memorial on Easter Sunday 1939, was one of the most significant events in American musical history.

One of the most influential and eminent women in American history, she is renowned for her tireless, lifelong devotion to the cause of women's suffrage, but was also actively involved in the two other leading reform movements of the nineteenth century—abolition and temperance. These movements had a tendency to overlap and interact with one another in a "physician—heal thyself" fashion, i.e., women were not allowed an active voice in the temperance unions, blacks couldn't join the suffrage organizations, etc. Reform the reformers, wheels within wheels—a perfect nurturing environment for a potent and high-powered visionary like Susan B. Anthony, who went forth armed with a high degree of stalwart determination and this battle cry: "Failure is Impossible!"

His given name was John Chapman, and he *was* a real person. He was born in Massachusetts sometime around 1774 and he died in Fort Wayne, Indiana sometime around 1845. Johnny Appleseed is a classic example of the historical figure, like Beowulf or Lancelot or Joan of Arc, who become deeply immersed in the realm of legend and folklore and create auras among themselves that make it difficult to differentiate between myth and reality, which phenomenon is especially unique in this young country. Other American examples are Mike Fink, John Henry, and Casey Jones, as well as a few twentieth century contributions which will probably include Pretty Boy Floyd and D.B. Cooper.

One of his biographers speculates there might be a scholar who will pop up sometime in the future and attempt to discredit Satchmo's contributions to popular music on the theory that such brilliance is impossible to achieve without formal training "in the subtleties of phrasing, intonation, and harmony." An interesting observation, and an interesting comment on the inability of the human race to comprehend and recognize pure and raw genius when it appears. Similar things were said of Shakespeare, by the way. Pops undoubtedly would have considered that hilarious, especially after partaking of the essence of certain medicinally beneficial exotic herbs, as was his habit.

La Josephine returned to the United States to perform with the Zeigfield Follies in 1936, but was soon back in France, and became a naturalized French citizen the next year. She served her adopted country during World War II, and was honored and respected by the French people for her patriotic and humanitarian work. Twenty thousand people attended her funeral in 1975.

Phineas Taylor Barnum was, contrary to popular opinion, no charlatan or con man, and perhaps has been just a little misunderstood owing to that famous "There's a sucker born every minute" quote. People didn't mind being gently grifted, he figured, as long as they got a decent deal for their entertainment dollar. He advertised Amazing Spectacles and Wondrous Attractions, and never failed to deliver.

Born on Christmas Day 1821 and "changed worlds" on Good Friday 1912, Clara Barton perfectly exemplified the unique abilities of women to recognize a societal need and to make great progress towards fulfilling it by applying a matrilineal philosophy and course of action in ways men are not even able to comprehend. To clarify this, it is important to understand that the majority of the Civil War generals adopted an attitude toward their wounded soldiers similar to the way a modern person deals with a tire that can't be repaired: "What good is that to me? Get rid of it." Clara Barton overcame enormous odds regarding the fulfillment of her life's work, and her qualities of compassion and humanitarianism seem almost evolutionary.

## Ambrose Bierce *September 1912* ............................... 35

Bitter Bierce, they called him, as well as 'the wickedest man in San Francisco.' The Devil's Dictionary is one of his better known works: 'Happiness, n. An agreeable sensation arising from contemplating the misery of another.' Had a hand for epitaphs, too: 'Hotten. Rotten. Forgotten.' In 1913 he strutted into Eternity when he got the notion to go down to Old Mexico to see what Pancho Villa was up to. He disappeared down there and as a result created a lasting American literary mystery, for his fate was never, from that day to this, discovered.

## Elizabeth Blackwell *August 1851* ............................... 37

Determination and perseverance caused her dream of being the first woman American medical doctor to be realized, and don't forget how prevalent that 'old boy' network was in those days, especially in medicine. She also graduated first in the otherwise all-male graduating class of 1849 at Geneva Medical College and, as a contemporary of Clara Barton, made significant progress in the development of the science of nursing on the Civil War battlegrounds.

## Andrew Carnegie *May 1911* ............................... 39

He was a tycoon, but not one of those robber barons or ruthless capitalists so prevalent in the time. As a matter of fact, Andrew Carnegie's beliefs concerning the moral and ethical obligations of wealth made a lot of other rich people nervous, especially when he stated his conviction that if a man dies in possession of excess wealth he dies in disgrace. J.P. Morgan bought his steel interests out in 1900 for around four hundred million dollars, and Carnegie spent the rest of his life literally giving it away, determined to leave the world a better place than he found it.

## Charlie Chaplin *November 1918* ............................... 41

"He is the one genius created by the cinema"—GEORGE BERNARD SHAW
"He is a document which already qualifies as an historical event"—BERTHOLD BRECHT
"He has revived one of the great arts of the ancient world"—WINSTON CHURCHILL
"He is the pantomimist sublime"—SARAH BERNHARDT
"He is a goddam ballet dancer"—W.C. FIELDS
"Who is Mr. Chaplin?"—MAHATMA GHANDI
"I am a citizen of the world"—CHARLIE CHAPLIN

## Samuel Langhorne Clemens *1889* ............................... 43

Mark Twain might be the greatest novelist this country's ever seen, but even if he ain't, I reckon that when the topic of conversation gets around to the greatest American novel you can just say "Huckleberry Finn" and be done with it. But oftentimes creative brilliance doesn't lend itself too well to everyday business dealings, and maybe that's why Mr. Clemens lost a whole hatful of dough on the Paige Typesetting Machine.

## William F. Cody *1883* ............................... 45

Buffalo Bill's Wild West Show, a spectacular extravaganza which featured an array of Western thrills which could have been seen in their reality just a few years previous, went on to national and international fame and, aside from being a worldwide sensation "...such as never was seen before," established show business traditions and principles that are still adhered to a hundred years later. Buffalo Bill was awarded the Congressional Medal of Honor in 1872, but it and 910 others were rescinded by an Army investigative board in 1916.

## George M. Cohan *September 1910* ............................... 47

He was born into show business, and not for one minute of his life did it ever get out of his blood. It can't be put any better than it was by one of his biographers who said that he accurately represented the "bulging national ego" of his times. Franklin Roosevelt awarded him a special medal of merit in 1942 for composing "Over There," which had become the anthem of the First World War.

## George Armstrong Custer *January 1876* ............................... 49

It sure is fashionable to beat up on the General's memory these days, but it should always be remembered that, unlike almost every other politician or treaty maker or military man of the era, he didn't lie to the Indians. The 7th Cavalry rode out of Fort Lincoln with one thing in mind, and it had nothing to do with politicking or touching the pen-that-writes-two-ways. He said he was there to fight, and fight he did, and getting thoroughly whipped makes no difference whatsoever. There's nothing a warrior understands better than that.

He didn't practice law to accumulate an enormous fortune, although money was an issue with him. Complex and maybe just a little bit contrary, Clarence sincerely believed a person's true mission is to make a difference, to change and improve the world they find themselves in. Could be that a few of our modern day lawyers should pay some heed to that. And he did love baseball.

She possessed a poetic vision that can only be called eternal, and is now considered by many to be the greatest American poet, man or woman. She usually dressed in white and very seldom left the house, but that's probably not the reason her works will still be discussed and contemplated a thousand years from now.

Never once did she have any doubt about what she was going to do, and never once did she let anything get in her way, least of all a dismal public school education, where all they would have done was try to discourage her from pursuing the mastery of dance as not being a proper thing for a proper young lady to do. She showed them. In her autobiography Isadora says her mother lived exclusively on iced champagne and iced oysters while she was pregnant with her. Maybe more mothers should think of that.

Amelia was what they used to call an aviatrix, and it's a curious point to ponder why that handle seems to fit her. Perhaps it's the sense of adventure and womanhood it conveys. It would hardly raise an eyebrow if a woman set out to fly around the world now, but that wasn't the case in 1936. And now she's immortal, firmly set in legend.

If you don't have anything to do some evening, try inventing a parlor game that involves describing a famous person with just one word. In the case of Wyatt Earp, the winning word would be 'tough.' And if the rules of the game allowed for two words, you could always say 'very tough.' He was covered with a mighty hard bark, all right, and during his career as lawman in those wild Kansas cow towns he made a habit of defusing situations involving any number of drunken, rowdy, armed, and dangerous Texas cowboys by sheer force of will, seldom even drawing his six-gun.

Her story isn't pretty, but it happened. On the surface it doesn't really seem to make sense that physical beauty would prove to be a hindrance to a serious acting career for a woman, and that's where it becomes a true feminist issue. Hollywood... what they did to her was obscene.

A writer in one of the musical biography collections said that his music was an 'imitation' of the minstrelsy and slave songs of the day, a boneheaded statement which couldn't be farther from the truth. Stephen Foster's genius and influence, originating in an era when singing was a popular and universal part of day to day life, has now spread worldwide. He has been compared to Robert Burns, and rightfully so. Alcohol killed Stephen Foster at the age of 37.

Since the peak of his black nationalist movement in the early 1920's, this country has gone through an inestimable amount of change regarding civil rights and racial equality. There have appeared any number of dynamic and forceful leaders, but nobody cut from quite the same cloth as Marcus Garvey. He was focused, effective, and determined, and that's probably why they imprisoned and deported him. Pure African blood ran through his veins.

Bold, wild, free, and Indian to the core, he ranged and raided through his natural homeland in a manner which would have made the ancient Goths and Vandals beam with pride. An incomprehensibly furious enemy to those who did him wrong, he could also show great measures of beneficence and compassion when it was justified, a fact seldom addressed by the typical histories, insistent as they are in their portrayals of the Apache as nothing but bloodthirsty savages. Never granted his request to return to Arizona, Geronimo died, still technically a prisoner of war, at Fort Sill in 1909.

The heartless economic times we live in have given rise to a new breed of moneychangers, but most of them seem to be mere babes in the woods compared to Jay Gould and his cronies. Think of it: no income taxes, minimal governmental regulations, no minimum wage, no labor unions, the dollar still based on the gold standard, and when a rich man needed votes he simply bought them. There's a verse from an old bindle-stiff song that seems to sum up the essence of the railroad barons, and it goes like this:

> *"Jay Gould's daughter said before she died,*
> *Father, fix the blinds so the bums can't ride.*
> *If ride they must, let 'em ride the rods,*
> *Let them put their trust in the hands of God...."*

A hundred years from now there will be another world which will have come along to replace the one we have now, and an enormous amount of our popular culture will be gone and forgotten. "This Land is Your Land" won't be, though. Indeed, there shouldn't be any doubt it will prove to be just as lasting as "Auld Lang Syne." Speaking of which, it's curious to note how often Woody is compared to Robert Burns, both true voices of the common people. Besides unparalleled musical and poetic genius, the most telling single attribute they shared was the minstrel's gift of being able to rejuvenate, reinterpret, and preserve the old songs that had come down through the folklore, instill them with pertinent social significance, and give them lasting life. And not, as Woody so aptly put it, "...in a sissy tone of voice...."

There's probably no single facet of modern American life that is taken for granted more than the basic rights of the worker. There was a time when the bosses valued a human life less than they did a pick handle, and during the days of the birth of the labor unions enormous struggles were undertaken to change that. Joe Hill was in the vanguard of that fight, and his sword was his songs, mighty powerful weapons in his hands. His last words, before being executed by the State of Utah on November 19, 1915, were "Don't mourn. Organize!"

> *I dreamed I saw Joe Hill last night*
> *alive as you or me*
> *says I, "but Joe, you're ten years dead"*
> *"I never died", says he*

There are a few key points about Lady Day's life and career that seem especially pertinent to the study of the impact and influence she had on jazz and popular music. One is the changing quality she presented to the camera, the way each individual photograph seems to reveal another entirely different side of her, almost a changeling. Another is the fact that she lived what she sang, and the haunting poignancy and pathos of so many of her standards remains an eloquent testimonial to her life experience.

"Billie Holiday was and still remains the greatest single musical influence on me."—FRANK SINATRA

Magic, Illusion, and Escapology require a high level of determination, dedication, and discipline to master as a craft, and Mr. Houdini evolved them to advanced forms of performance art. Fearless, confident, and bold, he became an international sensation, and published *A Magician Among the Spirits* and *Miracle Mongers and Their Methods* before his death on Halloween night 1926.

She isn't exactly a household name, but every second Sunday in May her legacy is reborn when mothers everywhere are honored and remembered. Anna Jarvis is a classic example of a person who discovered her mission in life and successfully pursued it, and upon contemplating her dedication and determination, it becomes apparent that Mother's Day was not created solely to sell greeting cards.

A supremely gifted black heavyweight boxer from a Southern state appears on the scene. He is impossibly quick on his feet for such a big man and possesses unbelievable power and a confusing array of moves. He taunts & mocks his opponents in the ring, is extroverted, outspoken, confident, loud, and arrogant outside of it, and does a bang-up job of assaulting the status quo. Public opinion ranges from unabashed adoration to vituperative condemnation, and is never lukewarm. He is persecuted by the racist establishment and brought up on various charges, but makes no apologies and remains proud and confident of who he is. Sound familiar? Sure, it could be Muhammad Ali, but this is Jack Johnson, who did his thing about fifty years before Muhammad. And by the way, who *was* the greatest heavyweight ever?

## Scott Joplin *September 1910* . . . . . . . . . . . . . . . . . . . . . . . . . . . . . . . . . . . . 83

Scott Joplin used the phrase 'Afro-American' in the first decade of this century, which fact should serve as an indication of how far ahead of his times he was. He enjoyed quite a measure of fame and success as the creator of ragtime music, but never lived to see his grand opera "Treemonisha" produced on the scale he envisioned. As so often happens, it took decades for his brilliance to be generally recognized, and it wasn't until the 1970's that the soundtrack of the movie "The Sting" launched his star.

## David Kalakaua *September 1881* . . . . . . . . . . . . . . . . . . . . . . . . . . . . . . . . . 85

They didn't call him the 'Merry Monarch' for nothing. In true Hawaiian fashion, he arranged it so that business & industry took a back seat to food, dance, and festivity on any conceivable occasion, and managed to have a riotous good time while reigning as King. He did, however, understand the importance of ensuring that the Islands played a pivotal role concerning the balance of power in the Pacific.

## Emmett Kelly *October 1937* . . . . . . . . . . . . . . . . . . . . . . . . . . . . . . . . . . . . 87

The Weary Willie character became the single most famous clown personification in the history of American circus. A true mud and truck show trouper, Emmett Kelly was on the road for years with numerous shows, developing and perfecting the character. Even his suit was seasoned to perfection, and is part of the memorabilia collection at the Emmett Kelly Museum in Sedan, Kansas, Emmett's home town.

## Queen Lydia Lili'uokalani *January 1893* . . . . . . . . . . . . . . . . . . . . . . . . . 89

She was the last of the long line of royalty in Hawai'i as the lineage faded away with the coming of the 20th Century. Modern times marched in and left no room for the splendor of the Ali'i of old, but modern times also meant new prosperity and positive progress for all Hawaiians, and Lili'uokalani knew it. It seems so fitting it was she, of pure royal Hawaiian blood, who would be the one chosen by the muses to write "Aloha Oe," the seamless and perfect signature song of the Islands.

## Jack London *December 1898* . . . . . . . . . . . . . . . . . . . . . . . . . . . . . . . . . . . 91

The essential restless adventurer, he went out into the world and acquired the best sort of education for a writer of his caliber. How else could he have created Wolf Larsen, the captain of the Sea Wolf, and all his other raw, wild, and brilliant literature? He certainly couldn't have done it if he had continued on as a swinkful professional laborer. An interesting footnote: He was influenced and encouraged in his creative endeavors by Ina Donna Coolbrith, the Oakland Public Library's visionary librarian, and so was Isadora Duncan.

## Huey Long *August 1935* . . . . . . . . . . . . . . . . . . . . . . . . . . . . . . . . . . . . . . . 93

It's hard to imagine that Huey Long would have defeated Franklin Roosevelt in the Presidential elections of 1936, but he was making a mighty strong run for it. By the middle of 1935 his Share-Our-Wealth movement was spreading like wildfire throughout the country, probably because the idea of equal distribution of wealth made a lot of sense to millions of Americans trudging through the fifth year of the Great Depression. We'll never know what he might have done, though, as a gunman's bullet put an end to all of it later that year.

## Juliette Gordon Low *October 1913* . . . . . . . . . . . . . . . . . . . . . . . . . . . . . . 95

If we are ever blessed with anything approaching wisdom, we may finally learn that true success is not measured by monetary or material gain, but rather by whether or not a person fulfilled the purposes of their life's mission and left a legacy which impacted and improved future generations. If this is true, then Juliette might be the most successful person who ever lived. Exuberant, enthusiastic, unique, funny, and perhaps a bit illogical, "…she loved that big hat and that ridiculous whistle."

## Aimee Semple McPherson *1926* (by Rolf McPherson and Timothy B. Doe) . . . . . . . . . 97

Sister was an evangelist in the old-time tradition, as well as a consummate and instinctive stage performer whose sermons were played to packed houses at the Angelus Temple in Los Angeles, where her spirit lives on to this day. In 1926 she was touched by a bit of scandal which grew to one of the biggest media events in Los Angeles history, and from which she emerged with her reputation not only unscathed, but enhanced. The Church of the Foursquare Gospel, based in Los Angeles, today has a membership of 2 million worldwide.

Herman Melville's story is interesting for a variety of reasons. He lived the adventurous life he wrote about— a better education a novelist can't ask for. After early initial success with his books, he went after a more stable and dependable career as a bureaucrat, which is a bit different from the way writers usually do things. He didn't lose his touch, though, and published "Billy Budd-Foretopman" late in life.

Those old graybeard fatcats in the War Department of the 1920's absolutely refused to believe aircraft would ever play a significant strategic role in modern warfare, even after they saw Mitchell's planes in a bombing demonstration sink a battleship in a matter of minutes. He was a true visionary who predicted the future with pinpoint accuracy, for which heinous act he was court martialed. It is a great pity he didn't live to see the attack on Pearl Harbor.

No, he didn't fight in China in the Boxer Rebellion, and no, he didn't break horses for the British in Africa during the Boer War, and no, he wasn't a Texas Ranger, nor a revenue agent in Tennessee. What he was, though, was a real cowboy, a true showman, and the greatest Western movie star of all time. Some might say the Duke gets that honor, and he is the biggest box-office draw ever, but if you want to talk purely Western, purely cowboy, the tip of the ol' ten-gallon goes to Tom. Generous, clean living, honest, and straight shootin', he was always the guy in the white hat.

He was an old man when he led the fight to save the Hetch Hetchy Valley, and it was a bitter defeat for him, one which undoubtedly hastened his death. Hetch Hetchy was a mini-Yosemite, and from the photographs and descriptions existing it's apparent it was one of the most stunning natural panoramic masterpieces in the West. It's drowned under hundreds of feet of water now, but that's progress.

Carry Nation was a temperance crusader, and made her rounds with a hatchet in one hand and a Bible in the other. She was, shall we say, rather steadfast in her belief that people shouldn't partake of intoxicating potations. This, shall we say, ironclad determination led to her establishing a bit of a reputation concerning the unique and unusual methods she used to present her opinions to the imbibing public. These methods— called 'hatchetations'—were, shall we say, quite respected in watering holes throughout Kansas and, boy, if you were in there having one and she came in through the front door you'd better know where that back door is—and you'd better know quick.

She used a .22 rifle for that remarkable sharpshooting (a choice trivia question), and remarkable it was, too. One of her better known tricks was to fill a playing card with holes as it fell through the air, and to this day an 'Annie Oakley' means a free pass in the parlance of travelling show business. Her skills impressed her future husband, a sharpshooter himself, enough to propose marriage. The Sioux on the Wild West Show were completely taken by her, and called her "Wan Tan Yeya Ci Sci La" (Little Sureshot).

A key player in what is arguably the single most significant and important scientific development in the history of civilization, his intellect was very lofty and difficult for ordinary people to comprehend. This had a lot to do with why the red-baiters went after him, that and the fact that Oppenheimer, like the vast majority of the physicists who developed the bomb, had serious reservations about their discoveries being perverted into the manufacture of super-weapons.

When he tried out for the Mobile Tigers, his first real team, the manager called him over after watching him pitch. "Do you do that constantly?" the manager asked. "No, sir," Satchel replied, "I do it all the time." By 1961 it was estimated that he had pitched around 2,500 games and had won more than 2,000 of them, including 300 shutouts and 55 no-hitters. Break out the calculator. And if that isn't enough to guarantee immortality, he also invented 'Satchel's Rules For Staying Young,' the most famous of which is: "Don't look back; something might be gaining on you."

When reviewing the performance of a well known actress in a Broadway production, Dorothy Parker wrote, "she ran the gamut of emotions from A to B." On her 70th birthday, she said "If I had any decency, I'd be dead.

Most of my friends are." And although its been quoted to nearly the point of ad nauseam, and attributed to God only knows who else, we have to remember her comment on the death of Calvin Coolidge, famous for his taciturnity: "How can they tell?"

His mother, a white woman, was kidnapped at the age of nine by Comanches and lived amongst them for years. When she was 'rescued' by Texas Rangers, she withered and died like a flower picked from the stem. His father was a war chief of the Quahadi band of the Comanche, and Quanah personified the best of both races. When it came time for the bankers and the money-grubbers to attempt to steal what little land the Indians had left Quanah stepped in and taught them a thing or two about effective business negotiations. They were surprised, to say the least.

In an enlightened society, the creative geniuses are taken care of and provided for as a consideration toward the collective common good, as well as for posterity. Poe, however, had to publish his first book at his own expense, no mean undertaking for someone with no money. That volume, by the way, is now one of the most, if not the most, valuable collector's items in American literary history.

A masterpiece of organization, logistical planning, and administration, the Pony Express lasted only eighteen months or so, but long enough to be firmly implanted in the annals of the West. Curious note: the rates were lowered as service was improved, which actually does make sense. Perhaps someone should bring that fact to the attention of Bell Telephone. The completion of the transcontinental telegraph line in October 1861 finished off the Pony Express, but not before its stalwart employees, "...daring young men, preferably orphans," rode into history.

When he travelled to Europe at the height of his fame the red carpet was literally rolled out for him. Huge crowds greeted him at every stop, and he was wholeheartedly accepted as a towering creative force, nearly a superman. Then he comes back to the United States and can't even get a Pullman berth on the train or a hotel room in New York City or a sandwich in a restaurant. Small wonder he considered the Russian culture advanced and civilized, and that was all the witch hunting McCarthyites needed to tear him down. That and the fact he was black.

There is nothing as purely and uniquely American as baseball, and that's why the Jackie Robinson story possesses such enormous historical and sociological significance. It is uplifting to contemplate the fact that the breaking of the color barrier in the Major Leagues has done more towards curing the disease of racism than has the weak-willed efforts of any number of ineffective 'social reformers' or self-centered misguided politicians. The fact that Jackie was an enormously gifted ballplayer had a lot to do with it, too.

A product of an era of optimism we certainly aren't privileged to enjoy, he was the embodiment of good will, humor, and vision, not to mention the first man in the world to lasso a wild zebra. Will was the kind of guy who could walk into a room and immediately elevate the general mood of the occasion simply by virtue of his presence. His worth was even recognized by politicians and the media and that, upon contemplation, will prove to be a rather stunning statement.

Personally, I am spending much time with the books of this guy. Furthermore, I am of the opinion indeed that all smart guys and dolls should do much the same thing, as I do not know of a more surefire fashion with which to become acquainted with the likes of Sky Masterson and Harry the Horse and Spanish John and Dave the Dude and Dream Street Rose and Angie the Ox and Nathan Detroit and Miss Missouri Martin and Twelve Gun Tweeny and Little Isadore and Sam the Gonoph and Mindy, all of whom I do now think much about, and highly of.

He pursued a myriad number of occupations before he hit it big with the chicken, which is an often repeated formula for success when you study the lives of people who have made it. The lesson that can be learned from the Colonel's story is that if the people are presented with a quality product at a fair price, with no games played or strings attached, they'll be back for more. More business should be done that way.

## Ignaz Schwinn *November 1936*

Among the host of other significant and worthwhile aspects of American culture and history that have been forgotten is the impact and influence the development of the bicycle had on the society. In 1902 there were two patent offices—one dealing with the bicycle industry and one dealing with everything else. It's phenomenal to contemplate how popular bicycling was at the turn of the century (albeit a rich man's game), and how rapidly it declined to the status of a kid's pastime. And what do you suppose we have to thank for that? That's right—that most marvelous miracle of the modern age, our friend, the motorcar.

## Sitting Bull *September 1889*

Sitting Bull was somewhere in his mid-40's by the time of the Battle of the Little Big Horn where he was the most significant and influential headman of the largest gathering of Plains Indians the North American continent had ever seen. He joined Buffalo Bill's Wild West Show in later years and toured for awhile, adapting fairly well to the changes that had swept across his country. But he never could quite understand why, in the midst of all the wealth and splendor of the modern Eastern cities, there could be people on the streets begging for bread. That type of poverty was a completely foreign concept to the Lakota.

## Jedediah Smith *1831*

Trailblazer, Explorer, and Mountain Man in the grand tradition, Jed Smith covered an enormous amount of Western territory after leaving New York State in 1818. A literate man, which set him somewhat apart from the majority of the mountain men of the early 19th century, he was rubbed out by a Comanche war party in 1831. One of the Indians who was there told the story to the traders at Santa Fe. Jed had two pistols and one musket (muzzle loaders, of course) and before they got him he killed three of the braves in the war party. 3 shots, 3 Indians—he died like a warrior and a true mountain man.

## Gertrude Stein *October 1934*

One of the better biographies of Gertrude Stein is called *Everybody Who Was Anybody*, a most appropriate title. An expatriate from Pennsylvania, she reigned over the Paris art and literary scene for decades like, as one acquaintance put it, "a great Jewish Buddha," and the guest list of 27 rue de Fleurus reads as a veritable who's who of painters, writers, poets, journalists, and philosophers of the time. Her final words were spoken to her lifelong friend and companion, Alice B. Toklas, as she was being wheeled into the operating room. She looked up at Alice and said, "What is the answer?" Receiving no reply, she said, "In that case, then what is the question?"

## Levi Strauss *April 1873*

Levi Strauss is a classic example of the totally unique qualities of the American entrepreneurial experience. The opportunities available in this country simply didn't exist in Europe, and hard work, a clear vision, and a definite need for an innovative, quality product were the ingredients of the formula for Levi's success. His reward was being able to watch his company prosper for the nearly fifty years he served as its president, all the while actively participating in a variety of philanthropic and benevolent endeavors.

## Billy Sunday *March 1917*

An old-fashioned preacher of the old-time religion, Billy Sunday was arguably the most influential evangelist this country's ever seen, and the model for every personification of the thundering revivalist preacher since. His tabernacle revivals grew to events of enormous popularity during the peak years of the First World War, and he lorded over them spewing torrents of fiery invective and rip-roaring brimstone which captivated his audiences and led to a phenomenal conversion rate. As a young man he had his first taste of fame as a speedy outfielder with the Chicago White Stockings and could round the bases from a standing start in 14 seconds.

## Nikola Tesla *January 1901*

Cellular telephones. Fax machines. Radar. Television. Lasers. Rural Electrification. Solar Energy. We have a tendency to take these technologies for granted in the modern times we live in, but what would you have said about them a hundred years ago? That's about the time Nikola Tesla theorized the feasibility of these modern realities. Maybe the most ambitious thing he could have done was perfect the method of wireless transmission of high voltage electricity, but we'll never know, for as support for his visionary projects waned he slid into eccentricity, a common enough fate for so many of the higher intellects.

## Jim Thorpe *1921*

Contrary to certain fashions of popular thinking, race was not the real issue when it came to Jim Thorpe being stripped of the Gold Medals he won at the 1912 Olympics. As a matter of fact, the American people were united in their support of him, and were proud of an American Indian whipping the world in track & field. But the International Olympic Committee is, and always has been, a very staid and proper organization, and stood by their guns for more than sixty years. Jim's records were reinstated in 1983.

One of the most universal rites of male American childhood has got to be the parental admonition which, in its essence, says "Be careful with that! You could put your brother's eye out doing that!" Well, that's exactly what happened to James Thurber at the age of six, while faithfully reenacting the William Tell saga. The left eye, it was. The injury eventually resulted in his being declared legally blind, and yet he went on to create some of the most brilliant line cartoons and drawings ever to grace the pages of the old *New Yorker*. And if further evidence of his creative genius is ever required, contemplate his response to an editor's demand that all news story leads be made as lean as possible: "Dead. That was what the man was the police found in an areaway last night."

Writer. Good one.

When it gets around to the subject of courage, you might as well just say 'Harriet Tubman' and let it go at that. After a bold and brilliant career as a conductor on the Underground Railroad, she served with great distinction in the Union Army during the Civil War, receiving a remarkable number of letters of commendation and testimonials from ranking Union officers in the process. But she still waited 30 years for a twenty dollar monthly pension, and received a grand total of two hundred dollars before her death.

Hank and Bill, as they're affectionately known within the organization, did business the old fashioned way. Which is to say they provided dependable, trustworthy service and guaranteed all losses would be reimbursed, promptly, to the shipper. Losses were an issue, too, for in the early days the highwaymen and bandits ran rampant throughout California and held up the coaches nearly at will. Things started to change in 1873, though, the year Jim Hume was hired as detective. He took to the job with great energy, and soon made things mighty warm for the desperados.

A true Bohemian, he would have liked you to believe he was born in St. Petersburg, but the truth of the matter is the happy event took place in not-quite-as-exotic Lowell, Massachusetts in 1834. He expatriated himself in the grand fashion, and like Isadora and La Josephine, never returned to live in the land of his birth. A clever wag who could whip Oscar Wilde in a battle of the wits, his most famous contributions to art history are "An Arrangement in Grey and Black," commonly known as "Whistler's Mother," and his book *The Gentle Art of Making Enemies*, published in 1890. The book was inspired by his victorious libel suit against the redoubtable art critic John Ruskin, who had vociferously condemned certain of Whistler's works, and for which he was awarded a settlement of one farthing.

# Marian Anderson

713 Colorado Street
Philadelphia, Pennsylvania
—or—
c/o Sol Hurok Production & Management
220 West 42nd Street
New York, New York

## Declaration of Intent

To secure a suitable location in the nation's Capitol for a concert of classical operatic arias, American Negro spiritual selections, and German lieder music tentatively scheduled to be performed on Easter Sunday next year.

## Artistic Vignette

Recognized at a very early age as being in possession of a vocal talent of a rare and exceptional order, her voice was developed and refined through extensive professional training and has evolved into a contralto of such power, clarity, and presence that audiences have been known to be stunned into silence and unable to applaud at the end of a performance. The extensive European concert engagements of 1930–1935 have established her Continental reputation as an artist of the highest caliber and greatest magnitude.

## Significant Concert Successes

- Lewisohn Stadium, New York, with the New York Philharmonic, August 1925
- English debut, Wigmore Hall, London, England, September 1930
- Bach Saal, Berlin, Germany, October 1930 (Rosenwald Fellowship)
- Scandinavian Tours, 1932–1933    • Russian Tours, 1935–1936
- Salle Gaveau, Paris, June 1934    • Salzburg, Austria, August 1935
- New York: Town Hall, New Year's Eve 1936; Carnegie Hall, January 1936

## Vocal & Repertoire Training

United States:
- Mary Saunders Patterson, Philadelphia  • Agnes Reifsnyder, Philadelphia
- Giuseppe Boghetti, Philadelphia  • Leon Rothier, New York  • Frank LaForge, New York

Europe:
- Raimund von Zur Mühlen  • Mark Raphael  • Amanda Ira Aldridge  • Sverre Jordan
- Michael Rauchisen  • Germaine de Castro  • Madame Charles Cahier

The Programs are now including works by Brahms, Dvorak, Handel, Pergolesi, Rachmaninoff, Rimsky-Korsakov, Schubert, Schuman, and Strauss as well as the spiritual compositions of Lawrence Brown, R. Nathaniel Dett, Roland Hayes, Hall Johnson, and Florence Price.

## Testimonial

"What I heard today one is privileged to hear only once in a hundred years."

—Arturo Toscanini, Hôtel de l'Europe, Salzburg, August 8, 1935, after a recital of *The Crucifixion*

# Susan B. Anthony

17 Madison Street
Rochester, New York

## Statement of Purpose & Intent

To generate publicity and public notice throughout the Nation regarding the recent arrest of the Suffragist on charges of casting a vote for a Congressional representative and to present the position that the constitutionally guaranteed right to vote extends to all women through liberal interpretation of the Fourteenth and Fifteenth Amendments.

## Encapsulated Biographical Synopsis

Devoted, energetic, & forthright Social Reformer dedicated to achieving the constitutionally guaranteed doctrines of equality regardless of sex, race, or creed for all citizens in all matters related to exercising basic rights as offered by the dictates of the Republic; refined & estimable, as well as unusually independent, the Agitator is an accomplished lyceum lecturer and possesses planning and organizational skills of the highest order.

## Organizations & Involvements

✦ New York State Agent/Emissary, American Anti-Slavery Society, 1856–1864—"No Union With Slaveholders! Overthrow This Government, commit its blood stained Constitution To The Flames...!"

✦ Adherent, Daughters of Temperance, 1849–1852—"Ladies! There Is No Neutral Position For Us To Assume..."

✦ Organizer, Women's New York State Temperance Society, 1852—Elizabeth Cady Stanton, President

✦ Participant, Women's Rights Convention, Syracuse, 1852; Whole World's Temperance Convention, New York City, 1853

✦ Organizer, Women's Loyal League; established 1863—dissolved 1864—"There Must Be A Law Abolishing Slavery!"

✦ Corresponding Secretary, American Equal Rights Association, formed 1866—"One Grand, Distinctive Idea—Universal Suffrage"

✦ Founder/Officer, National Woman Suffrage Association, organized 1869

✦ Organizer, Working Women's Association; Delegate, National Labor Union Convention, 1868—"Scorn To Be Coddled By Your Employers..."

✦ Publisher, "The Revolution," 1st Edition, January 1868—"Educated Suffrage Irrespective Of Sex And Color"

## Tutelage & Edification Commissions

▲ Schoolmarm, Eunice Kenyon's Friends' Seminary, New Rochelle, New York, 1839
▲ Schoolmistress, Center Falls District, Center Falls, New York, 1840
▲ Headmistress (Female Division), Canajoharie Academy, Rochester, New York, 1846–1849

## Prominent & Notable Reformers
### Who Will Assuredly Provide Propitious Testimonials

✦ Elizabeth Cady Stanton ✦ Wendell Phillips ✦ Amelia Bloomer ✦ Lucretia Mott
✦ Frederick Douglass ✦ Lucy Stone ✦ William Lloyd Garrison ✦ George Francis Train

# Johnny Appleseed

c/o POSTMASTER
FORT WAYNE, INDIANA

## PROCLAMATION OF ULTIMATE PURPOSE & INTENT

NOW NEARING THE END OF HIS WORLDLY JOURNEYS, IT IS THE INTENTION OF THE ARBORIST TO EDUCATE THE POPULACE AS TO THE BENEFICIAL PURSUITS OF POMOLOGY AND TO ENSURE THAT THE GOOD WORD OF THE MERITS OF THE APPLE BE SPREAD, IN PERPETUITY, THE WIDTH AND BREADTH OF THIS GREAT NATION.

## SUMMARIZED DELINEATION OF CHARACTERISTICS

The nation-important work of the notionatin' man-o-dreams and American John the Baptist is not done even though, as of this late date, apple orchards bloom and thrive throughout the State of Pennsylvania, the Ohio Valley, along the Wabash, through the cricks, rivers, reaches, & runs of the Mohican Valley, along the Tiffin & Maumee Rivers and the shores of Lake Erie, the Valley of the Walholding, on the banks of the Monongahela, within the Firelands, and deep into the trackless wilds of the Western Wilderness. Of the Swedenborgian faith, he is angelic, ethereal, unworldly, and shyly eloquent; the true & real friend of all the creatures of the forest as well as independent of corporal wants, sufferings, and material needs; ever in the habit of traveling foot-naked and always held in the highest esteem by all who chance by his poor pindlin' self. Revered, respected, and protected by the Indians, he counts among his Red brethren the great braves & patriarchs Blue Jacket, Seneca John, Jim Jerk, Billy Mature, Captain Pipe, Kilbuck, Walk-in-the-Water, and Tarhe the Crane.

## BREVILOQUENT HISTORIETTE OF PERSONAL PARTICULARS

• *Born during Apple-Cider Time, 1774, Leominster, Massachusetts Bay Colony* • *Baptized at the Congregational Meeting, 1775* • *Family established residence at Longmeadow, 1777* • *Schooled and versed in the Scriptures, the Dilworth Speller, and the New England Primer* • *Employed as Orchardist, Susquehanna Region, Pennsylvania, 1790s* • *Various missionatin's in the Potomac country* • *First frontier planting at Big Brokenstraw Creek, County of Warren*

## ORCHARD ESTABLISHMENTS AND OTHER ARBOREAL ENDEAVORS

- On the Sandusky River
- Brunersburg
- Wayne's War Road
- Indian Fork
- Muskingum Valley
- Shanesville
- Mifflin
- Belpré
- Chillicothe
- Wheeling

## OMNIUM-GATHERUM OF APPLE VARIETIES

The Roxbury Russett • Winter and Golden Pippins • Red Gillyflower • French Paradise • Nonesuch • The Red Astrachan • Fall Wine • Bellflower • Early Harvest • Fallawater • Willow Twig • Front Door • Putnam Sweet • The Sweet Bough • Rambos • Seek-No-Further • Never–Fail

# Louis Armstrong
### 33rd Street & Cottage Grove
### Chicago, Illinois

• • • • • • • • • • • • • • • • • • • • • • • • • • • • • • • • • • • • • • • • • • • • • • • • • • • •

## Aspiration & Ambition

To organize, form, and otherwise establish a studio jazz band that will consist of, but not be limited to, cornet, trombone, piano, saxophone, and drums, and is tentatively to be called the "Hot Five," or, as the situation warrants, the "Hot Seven."

## Profile of Noteworthy Characteristics

Energetic, lively, and capable young cornetist in possession of a remarkably wide array of musical talents as well as a pronounced enthusiasm and eagerness regarding the dissemination of the medium of jazz to a broad and diverse audience. Innovative and distinctive subtleties of timing, executions, styles, and phrases, together with a readily apparent mastery of bold and revolutionary licks, codas, breaks, interpolations, leaps, deliveries, instrumental voicings, "scattings," and improvisations all bear eloquent and resonant testimony to the peerless gifts of a significant young talent at the prelude of a stellar career.

## Significant Musical Influences

♪ Early quartet singing on the streets of New Orleans with Little Mack, Big Nose Sidney, Redhead Happy Bolton; the traditional ragtime of Buddy Bolden, Joe "Cornet" Oliver, Bunk Johnson, and Freddy "Cornet" Keppard

♪ The Creole music of Celestine, Alphonse Picou, Emmanuel Perez, "Papa" Laine, and Bouboule Augustin

♪ Instruction received from Captain Joseph Jones & Professor Peter Davis at the Colored Waif's Home, New Orleans (tambourine, snare drum, bugle, alto horn, cornet), 1913–1914

♪ The clubs, dance halls, and cabarets of New Orleans including Henry Ponce's, Spano's, the Funky Butt Hall, Savocca's, Matranga's, Pete Lala's, the Franc Amis Hall, the Economy, the Co-Operative Hall, and others

## Partial Historiette of Earlier
## Horn-Playing Situations & Engagements

### New Orleans & St. Louis:

• Henry Matranga's Tavern, Perdido Street, 1917–1918 • Kid Ory's Band (Pete Lala's, Co-operative Hall, etc.), 1919 • Fate Marable's Band aboard Streckfus Line riverboats *Sydney* and *Saint Paul*, May 1919–September 1921 • Tom Anderson's Cabaret Club • Silver Leaf Band • Oscar Celestin's Tuxedo Band • Zutty Singleton's Trio (Fernandez Club)

### Chicago:

• King Oliver's Creole Jazz Band, (second cornet), Lincoln Gardens, 1923–1924 (first recordings made 3/23) • Ollie Power's Band, Dreamland, 1924 • Lil Armstrong's Dreamland Syncopators, 1925

### New York:

• Fletcher "Smack" Henderson's 12-Piece Orchestra, Roseland Ballroom, September 1924–November 1925 (five-state summer tour, 1925)

# Josephine Baker
Villa Le Beau-Chêne
Le Vésinet, France

## Déclaration d'Intention

*T*o return to the United States, after 10 years popular success in France, and embark on a theatrical tour with the intention of illuminating the American people as to the daring, bold, and avant-garde qualities of modern European musical revue entertainment.

## Biographie Courte

*A*udacious, elevated, and elegant, *La Josephine* has, by virtue of her colossal and unequaled talent, taken Paris by storm since her debut with the Revue Nègre at the Théâtre des Champs-Élysées in October 1925. The *con anima* personification of primitive eroticism and savage grace & sensuality, she embodies a living return to the seasons of the childhood of man by advancing her completely unique dance methods to levels of artistic style & power never before witnessed on any civilized stage.

## Histoire Premièrement

✳ Born June 6, 1906, St. Louis, Missouri; first employed as waitress at the Old Chauffeur's Club, Pine Street, St. Louis

✳ Performed with the Jones Family Band on the street outside the Booker T. Washington Theatre; first stage appearance with the Dixie Steppers, 1919

✳ Toured with the Theatre Owners' Booking Association, 1920–1921

✳ Chorus line, *Shuffle Along*, Sissle/Blake/Miller/Lyle producers, 1921–1924

✳ Chorus Line/Featured, Sissle & Blake's *Chocolate Dandies*, 1924–1925

✳ Dancer, Plantation Club, New York, 1925

## Succèses l'Europe

➹ Revue Nègre, Théâtre des Champs-Élysées, avenue Montaigne, Paris; Nelson Theatre, Kurfürstendamm, Berlin; Brussels

➹ Folies Bergère, *La Folie du Jour*; *La Revue des Revues*, European tours

➹ Opened Chez Josephine Night Club, Paris, December, 1926; World Tour, 1928

➹ Casino de Paris, *Paris Qui Revue*, 1930; *La Joie de Paris*, 1931

➹ Films: *La Sirène des Tropiques*, 1927; *Zou-Zou*, 1934; *Princesse Tam-Tam*, 1935

➹ Autobiographies: *Mémoires de Josephine Baker*; *Une Vie de Toutes les Couleurs*

➹ Notable songs: "La Petite Tonkinoise" • "J'ai Deux Amours" • "Voulez-vous de la Canne à Sucre" • "Dis-nous, Josephine" • "Pretty Little Baby" • "Suppose" • "Bye Bye Blackbird" • "I Love Dancing" • "I'm Just Breezing Along with the Breeze"

➹ Ballet training with George Balanchine

**"She is the Nefertiti of Now."**—*Pablo Picasso*

"J'ai deux amours, mon pays et Paris
Par eux toujours, mon couer est ravi."

Eng. by H. Iret from a Dag.by Ros.

# PHINEAS TAYLOR BARNUM

c/o The American Museum
Corner of Broadway and Ann Street
New York City

---

## STATEMENT OF INTENT

To debunk the Humbugs, Mountebanks, Queer Plungers, and Naysayers as pertains to the Recognized Authenticity and Veritable Bonafide Value to the Public of New and Fantastic Marvels and Attractions Currently Exhibited at Mr. Barnum's American Museum, viz.:

✪ *The Great Model of Niagara Falls with Real Water!* ✪ *The Hope of the Family!*
✪ *The Prince of Serpents!* ✪ *The Wild Man of the Woods!* ✪ *The Creation!* ✪ *The Deluge!*
✪ *Anna, or the Child of the Wreck!* ✪ *The Woolly Horse!* ✪ *The Bearded Lady!*
✪ *Albinos!* ✪ *Giraffes!* ✪ *Giants!* ✪ *Freaks!* ✪ *Improbable Animals!*

*A Family of Industrious Fleas Trained in All Manners of Acrobatic Marvels!*
All which follow the Astounding Successes and Verified Authenticity of:
✺ Joice Heth, 160-Year-Old Nursemaid to the Father of the Country! ✺
✺ The Feejee Mermaid, Astounding Evolutionary Wonderwork! ✺
✺ The Thrilling & Astonishing Great Western Buffalo Hunt! ✺
✺ The Siamese Double Boys! ✺

**As Attested to by the Grateful and Delighted Denizens of Gotham:**
GENERAL TOM THUMB, THE CELEBRATED DWARF OF ELEVEN, JUST ARRIVED FROM ENGLAND!!!

---

## A BRIEF COMPENDIUM OF MR. P. T. BARNUM'S ILLUSTRIOUS & ILLUMINATIVE CAREER

☞ **Merchant** ☞ **Lottery Agent** ☞ **Boardinghouse Proprietor** ☞ **Porterhouse Keeper**
☞ **Editor** ☞ **Publisher** ☞ **Journalist** ☞ **Cattle Drover** ☞ **Bank President**
&

*Secretary, Treasurer, and Ticket Seller with the Old Columbian Circus of Aaron Turner*

---

*Mr. Barnum wishes it a matter of public knowledge that he and a select troupe are soon to embark on a journey to the Continent, there to be feted and toasted in splendor by the Crowned Heads of Europe, which shall include Queen Victoria, The Prince of Wales, King Leopold of the Belgians, The Dowager Queen Adelaide, King Louis Philippe, Queen Isabella of Spain, &c.*
*A most glorious and splendid source of Yankee pride is he!*
*All hats off to Mr. Barnum!*

### TESTIMONIALS AVAILABLE FROM:
• MOSES KIMBALL, BOSTON MUSEUM • DR. GRIFFIN, LYCEUM OF NATURAL HISTORY, LONDON

# *Clara Barton*

Ferguson House
1326 I Street, Northwest
District of Columbia

## Declaration of Purpose

To convince and persuade the Government of the United States and the American People to create, ratify, and otherwise establish a National humanitarian organization inspired and influenced by the International Red Cross, created at the Geneva Convention in August 1864 by the mutual agreement of 26 civilized nations, and to emulate the wisdom of its principles, the good practical sense of its details, and its extreme usefulness in practice.

## Conspectus of Characteristics

The "Angel of the Battlefield," the "Soldier's Friend," and "Florence Nightingale of America" is held in the highest esteem by compassionate and humanitarian people in all civilized lands for the sympathetic, commiserative, and benevolent services performed to alleviate the suffering of the myriad unfortunate wounded young stalwarts on many of the bloodstained battlefronts and arenas of conflict during the War Between the States. Determined, dedicated, and forthright, she has also proven to be somewhat impatient and obstinate when furthering the designs of her most singular and worthwhile cause.

## Concise Biographical Epitome

✦ Born Christmas Day, 1821, North Oxford, Massachusetts, into a family of scholars and teachers; received beneficial and progressive home education ✦ Boarded with Col. Richard C. Stone and attended the Oxford High School ✦ Philosophy, astronomy, Latin, and chemistry studies, Lucian Burleigh's School, Oxford ✦ Significant educational influence provided by L. N. Fowler and his book *Mental Science, as Explained by Phrenology* ✦ Formal schooling: Liberal Institute, Clinton, New York

## Professional Engagements & Occupations

➨ **Schoolteacher**, North Oxford, Charlton, West Millbury, &c., 1839–1850
➨ **Established Free Public School**, Bordentown, New Jersey, 1852
➨ **Government Clerk**, U.S. Patent Office, Washington, D.C. 1854–1857 (One of the first permanently appointed female Civil Servants; re-assigned 1860)

## Encapsulated Summary of Humanitarian Services Related to Relief and Succor Provided to the Union Cause While Following the Cannon During the Conflict Between the States

<u>Nurse, Cook, Supply Warden, and General Amanuensis</u>: Cedar Mountain (Manassas), August 1862 ✦ Second Battle of Bull Run, August 1862 ✦ Chantilly, August 1862 ✦ Antietam, September 1862 ✦ First Fredericksburg, December 1862 ✦ Siege of Charleston, April 1863 ✦ Battery Wagner (Morris Island), July 1863 ✦ Second Fredericksburg (Wilderness Campaign), May 1864
<u>Supervisor of Diet & Nursing</u>: Army Hospital, Point of Rocks, Virginia, 1864–1865
<u>Participant</u>: Andersonville Prison Grave Identification Mission, Georgia, July–August 1865
<u>Organizer</u>: Office of Correspondence with Friends of the Missing Men of the U.S. Army, 1865
<u>Lyceum Speaker</u>: "Work and Incidents of Army Life," "Scenes on the Battlefield," &c., 1866–68

## European Ministrations

International Red Cross Volunteer Nurse: Franco-Prussian War, 1870–1871

# Ambrose Bierce

**Olympia Apartments, 14th and Euclid Streets, N.W.**
**Washington, D.C.**

## Notice of Intent & Purpose

A diagonal journey (NE to SW) on the Mexican side of the Rio Grande to observe and report on the attractive unpleasantries currently being conducted down there between the them-that-own and the them-that-don't with the intent of sending in bulletins mostly false, of events mostly unimportant.

## Epitome

A disagreeable boyhood spent in boundless, grinding poverty on a malarious midwestern stump farm led to a premature loss of faith in nihilism and the cultivation of a healthy loathing for all but one member of the large family, encouraged, no doubt, by the father, who had detested *his* entire family as well. These factors, coupled with a rare inborn literary talent of the highest order, provided a fertile breeding ground for the enormous wealth of bitter homilies, acrimonious rondelets, pizenous parables, hebdomadal causeries, vehement anecdotes, phantasmal tales, vituperative villanelles, and the host of other choice scurrilities that have sprung from his most prolific pen over the past five decades.

## Military Service — War Between the States

Union Army Officer, Company C, 9th Indiana Infantry, 1861–1865; cited for bravery on several occasions; saw heavy action at Shiloh, Corinth, Chickamauga, and Chattanooga; wounded at Kennesaw Mountain; served with Gen. W. D. Hazen.

## Literary Dictatorships & Dissections

- **San Francisco:** THE NEWS LETTER, "Town Crier" & "Telegraphic Dottings" columns; Editor, 1868–1871
  - THE ARGONAUT, "Prattler" column; Editor, 1876–1878
  - THE WASP, Editor, 1880–1886
  - "The Haunted Valley," published in OVERLAND MONTHLY, 1871
  - Columnist, SAN FRANCISCO EXAMINER
- **London:** Staff Writer, FUN, 1872 • Editor, Mortimer's FIGARO, 1872–1873
  - Editor, HOOD'S COMIC ANNUAL, 1874 • Published THE FIEND'S DELIGHT, 1875
  - Editor, Empress Eugenie's LANTERN, 1875
- **Washington, D.C.:** Correspondent/Political Reporter, NEW YORK AMERICAN, 1899–1909
  - Columnist, "The Passing Show," COSMOPOLITAN, 1905–1906

## Partial List of Publications

\* Write It Right, **1909** \* The Shadow on the Dial, **1909** \* The Cynic's Work Book (The Devil's Dictionary), **1906** \* Shapes of Clay, **1903** \* Fantastic Fables, **1899** \* Can Such Things Be?, **1893** \* Black Beetles in Amber, **1892** \* Tales of Soldiers and Civilians, **1891** \* The Dance of Death, **1877** \* Cobwebs from an Empty Skull, **1874** \* The Fiend's Delight **(pseudonym: Dod Grile)**, **1872**

## Character References Available From:

- Brigadier General Jupiter Doke • Halpin Frayser • Peyton Farquhar • Joram Tate

# Elizabeth Blackwell, M.D.

44 University Place
Washington Square, New York City

---

## Notice of Intent to Establish Medical Practice

Miss Elizabeth Blackwell, M.D., recently returned from more than two years of study and practice on the Continent, wishes it known that she has opened a clinic at the above address and is prepared to practice in every department of her profession.

## Pertinent Biographical Information

- Born February 3, 1821, in Counterslip, near Bristol, England—Emigrated to United States, 1832
- Teacher, The Blackwell School, Cincinnati, Ohio, 1838–1844
- Teacher, Henderson School, Henderson, Kentucky, 1844–1845
- Music Teacher/Medical Student, Rev. John Dickson's School, Asheville, N.C., 1845–1847
- Medical Student, Dr. Joseph Allen's Philadelphia School of Anatomy, 1847
- Admitted to study at Philadelphia Hospital (Blockley Almshouse), Summer 1848

*Medical School:*

- *Rejections* by University of New York City • New York College of Physicians and Surgeons • Jefferson Medical College • Harvard • Yale • Bowdoin College • Vermont • Albany • University of Pennsylvania
- *Accepted* by Geneva Medical College (Student #130), Geneva, New York, October 1847
  Received Medical Degree, January 1849 (Graduated first in class)

## European Studies and Internships

✪ *Queen's Hospital, Birmingham* ✪ *General Hospital, Birmingham* ✪ *Consumption Hospital, London* ✪ *Obstetrical Collection of the Hunterian Museum, London* ✪ *St. Thomas, London* ✪ *La Maternité, Paris* ✪ *Guy's Hospital, Southwark* ✪ *St. Bartholomew's Hospital, London*

## Principal Professional Influences

- The significant medical contributions and advances made by women practitioners and healers in the societies of the ancient Chinese, Siamese, Assyrians, Egyptians, Greeks, and Romans.
- The three great medical schools, attended by women as well as men, during the reign of Queen Hatshepsut of Egypt.
- Hygeia and Panacea, daughters of Aesculapius; Pythias, wife of Aristotle; and the wife and daughter of Pythagoras.
- Medical laws enacted in Europe during the 7th, 8th, and 9th centuries, which included and protected women physicians as well as the significant contributions of Jewish and Arabian women during the Crusades.
- Dorothea Bocchi, Allesandra Giliani, Laura Bassi, and Anna Morandi Manzolini, medical graduates of the University of Bologna; Maria delle Donne, appointed Professor of Obstetrics and member of the French Academy of Sciences by Napoleon Bonaparte.

## A Tabulation of Individuals Willing to Testify to the High Degree of Miss Blackwell's Character and Professionalism

✤Florence Nightingale, Embley Park, Surrey, England
✤Horace Greeley, Editor, *New York Tribune*, New York, New York
✤Lady Noel Byron, widow of the poet, London
✤Sir John Herschel, c/o Royal Astronomical Society, London
✤Harriet Beecher Stowe, Brunswick, Maine

# Andrew Carnegie

2 EAST NINETY-FIRST STREET
NEW YORK, NEW YORK

## *Proclamation of Purpose*

To establish a Foundation or Corporation to promote the advancement and diffusion of knowledge and understanding among the people of the United States, by aiding technical schools, institutions of higher learning, libraries, scientific research, hero funds, useful publications, and such other agencies and means as shall from time to time be found appropriate therefore.

## *Encapsulated Conspectus of Sum & Substance*

A philanthropist with a deep commitment to furthering the causes of social betterment as well as a true Titan of modern industry and the first great leader of the Age of Steel, he is currently in his tenth year of retirement. In possession of unequaled moral and ethical standards related to firm beliefs regarding the obligations of great wealth, all energies are presently directed toward activities of donative largess, social altruism, and philanthropy on a grand scale. Representative list of related accomplishments to date include:

### *Trusts:*

*United States:*
- ➤ Carnegie Institute of Pittsburgh • 1896
- ➤ Carnegie Institution of Washington • 1902
- ➤ Hero Fund Commission • 1904
- ➤ Carnegie Foundation for the Advancement of Teaching • 1905
- ➤ Endowment for International Peace • 1910

*Europe:*
- ➤ Trust for the Universities of Scotland • 1901
- ➤ Dunfermline Trust, Scotland • 1903
- ➤ Hero Fund, Great Britain • 1908
- ➤ Temple of Peace, The Hague, Netherlands

### *Libraries (Partial list to 1899):*

❏ Bellevue Hospital Library, New York ❏ Johnstown Library ❏ Greensburg Library ❏ Carnegie (Pennsylvania) Library ❏ Washington Library ❏ Pennsylvania State College Library ❏ Edinburgh Library ❏ Dunfermline Library ❏ Aberdeen Library ❏ Inverness Library ❏ Jedburgh Library ❏ Dumfries Library ❏ Peterhead Library ❏ Sterling Library ❏ Wick Library

## *Brief Summation of Employment & Business History*

• **Messenger Boy/Operator**, Ohio Telegraph Co., Pittsburgh, Pa., 1850–1853 • Pennsylvania Railroad, 1853–1865—**Clerk/Operator**, 1853–1859; **Superintendent**, 12/59–3/65

• *Business endeavors:* Woodruff Sleeping Car Company • Pullman Palace Car Co. • Columbia Oil Company • Storey Oil Farm • Keystone Bridge Company • Superior Rail Mill • Pittsburgh Locomotive Works • Union Iron Mill • Homestead Steel Works • Carnegie Steel Company

## *Publications*

• *Round The World,* 1879 • *Our Coaching Trip,* 1880 • *An American Four-In-Hand in Britain,* 1883
• *Triumphant Democracy; or, Fifty Years' March of the Republic,* 1886 • *The Gospel of Wealth,* 1886
• *How to Get Rich,* **N.Y. Tribune,** 1891

Variable Distortograph, ca. 1927

# Charlie Chaplin

1416 North La Brea
Hollywood, California         -or-         2010 DeMille Drive
                                          Hollywood, California

## PROPOSED NATURE OF CINEMATIC CONSOCIATION

To form a motion picture production syndicate in cooperation with several well-known cinematic luminaries, united together as artists, with the express intent of producing and distributing quality moving pictures domestically and internationally.

## EPITOME OF ARTISTIC ATTRIBUTES & RENOWN

Internationally celebrated film director, writer, & star and acknowledged master of comedic styles characterized by a distinctive inner whimsicality and a sublime irreverence toward any and all pompous, self-important, or vainglorious institutions or societal standards as well as a pronounced sympathy and unshrouded compassion for the down-trodden, the meek, and the less fortunate, which affectations are quite prominent in his most gifted and moving portrayals of the "Little Tramp."

## PARTIAL INVENTORY OF FILMS TO DATE

**Keystone Film Company:** *1,2,6, & split reels (1914):* • Making a Living • Kid Auto Races at Venice • The Star Boarder • A Busy Day • Her Friend the Bandit • The Knockout • Mabel's Busy Day • Laughing Gas • The Face on the Barroom Floor • Dough and Dynamite • His Musical Career • Tillie's Punctured Romance • Getting Acquainted

**Essanay Company:** *2 & 4 reelers (1915–1916):* • His New Job • A Night Out • The Champion • A Jitney Elopement • The Tramp • By the Sea • Work • A Woman • The Bank • Shanghaied • A Night in the Show • Police • Carmen • Triple Trouble •

**Mutual Company:** *2 reelers (1916–1917):* • The Floorwalker • The Fireman • The Vagabond • One A.M. • The Count • The Pawnshop • Behind the Screen • The Rink • Easy Street • The Cure • The Immigrant • The Adventurer

**First National Film Company** *(1918–Present):* • A Dog's Life (3 reels) • Shoulder Arms (3 reels) • The Bond (½ reel) • Sunnyside (3 reels)

## EARLIER VAUDEVILLE & THEATRICAL ENGAGEMENTS & EMPLOYMENTS

■ Clog-Dancer, "Eight Lancashire Lads," 1899 ■ *Cinderella*, **The Hippodrome, London, 1900–1901** ■ **Blackmore's Theatrical Agency, 1902** ■ *Jim A Romance of Cockayne* (**Rôle: Sam, the Newspaper Boy**), 1903 ■ **William Gillette's** *Sherlock Holmes & the Painful Predicament of Sherlock Holmes* (**Rôle: Billy**), 1903–1905 ■ *Casey's Court Circus*, 1905 ■ **Six years with the dumb-show comedy compendium of Fred Karno: England:** *London Suburbia* ■ *The Football Match* ■ *Mumming Birds* ■ *The G.P.O.* ■ *The Yap–Yaps* ■ *Skating* ■ *Jimmy the Fearless; or, the Boy 'ero* ■ **New York Stage and Sullivan & Considine Circuit Tours:** *The Wow-Wows* ■ *A Night in an English Music Hall*

## SCHOOLING

• Victory Place Board School, Walworth, London, 1893–1894
• Hanwell Schools for Orphans and Destitute Children, London, June 1896–January 1898

# Samuel Langhorne Clemens

351 Farmington Avenue                                    Hartford, Connecticut

## Situation Sought

A station in a suitable situation of employment that would stand to benefit from the fanciful application of the remarkable and renowned creative abilities of this literary luminary, but not novel writing, for reasons best explained in the words of one of his most notable characters: "…if I'd 'a' knowed what a trouble it was to make a book I wouldn't 'a' tackled it, and ain't a-going to no more."

## Summation of Characteristics

This writer sees no need to elaborate on this angle, for if the reader doesn't know who Mr. Mark Twain is by now, the reader must have spent the better part of his days in a packing crate, or maybe Denver, and as such is of no use to my client anyhow.

## Major Works to Date (Partial List)

**Novels:**
* *The Adventures of Tom Sawyer* (1876)
* *The Prince and the Pauper* (1881)
* *The Adventures of Huckleberry Finn* (1884)
* *A Connecticut Yankee in King Arthur's Court* (to be published later this year)

**Travel Narrations & Reminiscences:**
* *The Innocents Abroad; or, The New Pilgrim's Progress* (1869)
* *Roughing It* (1872)
* *A Tramp Abroad* (1880)
* *Life on the Mississippi* (1883)

**Short Sketches and Tales:**
* *The Celebrated Jumping Frog of Calaveras County, and Other Sketches* (1867)
* *Mark Twain's Sketches, New and Old* (1875)
* *The Stolen White Elephant and Other Stories* (1882)

## Brief Employment History

* *Printer's Apprentice*, Hannibal, Missouri, 1848
* *Journeyman Printer*, St. Louis/New York City, 1853–1855
* *Steamboat Pilot Apprentice*, 1857–1859 (Licensed 1859)
* *Writer*, *Territorial Enterprise*, Virginia City, Nevada Territory, 1861–1864
* *Traveling Correspondent*, the *Alta California*, the *Sacramento Union*, and the *New York Tribune*, 1866–1869
* *Partner*, *Buffalo Express*, Buffalo, New York, 1870–1871

## Addendum

Currently engaged in the development, promotion, and eventual distribution of the Paige Typesetting Machine, a revolutionary and thoroughly advanced device sure to have a meritorious effect on the printing industry as well as all but guarantee a substantial financial return for all those fortunate enough to become involved in its development at an early date.

# William F. "Buffalo Bill" Cody
## Rural Route 1
## North Platte, Nebraska

## Purpose and Intent

To secure sponsorship and support for proposed theatrical extravaganza tentatively entitled "Buffalo Bill's Wild West Show and Congress of Rough Riders."

## Highlights of Expertise

☆ Eagle-Eyed *Scout & Guide*       ☆ Fearless & Daring *Indian Fighter*

☆ Unerring *Rifle & Pistol Shot*    ☆ Expert *Buffalo Hunter*

☆ Veteran *U.S. Army Trooper*       ☆ Successful *Theatrical Producer*

☆ ***Trailblazer, Plainsman, Pioneer, and Expeditionary*** ☆

## Chronicle of Employment

- **Cavvy Boy**, Expedition against the Mormons, 1857
- **Messenger**, Russell, Majors & Waddell, 1857
- **Pony Express Rider**, Russell, Majors & Waddell, 1860
- **Jayhawker**, Fort Leavenworth, Kansas, 1861
- **Scout**, 9th Kansas Cavalry (Kiowa & Comanche Expeditions), 1863
- **Scout**, General A. J. Smith, 1864
- **Buffalo Hunter**, Goddard Bros. (Kansas & Pacific Railway), 1867–1868
- **Chief of Scouts**, U.S. Army 5th Cavalry (seven expeditions & nine Indian fights)

## Noteworthy Accomplishments

🪶 Medal of Honor recipient, May 1872       🪶 First President, Showman's League of America

🪶 Guided Gen. G. A. Custer, Spring 1867    🪶 Guided Earl of Dunraven hunt, 1867

🪶 Guided Grand Duke Alexis hunt, 1872      🪶 Established Rome, Kansas, 1867

🪶 Killed Yellow Hair, Warrior, 1876        🪶 Killed 4,280 buffalo

🪶 Degree of Master Mason, January 1871

## Partial List of Publications
## Detailing Exploits & Career

*William F. Cody, Known as Buffalo Bill, the Famous Hunter, Scout, and Guide: An Autobiography*, 1879

*The Crimson Trail; or, Custer's Last Warpath, A Romance Founded Upon the Present Border Warfare, as Witnessed by Hon. W. F. Cody*, **N.Y. Weekly**, 1876

*Buffalo Bill's Best Shot; or, The Heart of Spotted Tail*, by Ned Buntline, 1872

*Buffalo Bill, King of the Border Men*, **N.Y. Weekly**, 1869

## Theatrical Endeavors

**Lead Role**, *The Red Right Hand; or, Buffalo Bill's First Scalp for Custer*, 1876

**Lead Role**, *The Knight of the Plains; or Buffalo Bill's Best Trail* and *May Cody; or, Lost and Won*, 1878–1879

**Producer**, *Scouts of the Prairies*, Ned Buntline, Author, and starring Texas Jack Omohundro and Wild Bill Hickock. Opened at Nixon Amphitheater, Chicago, December 16, 1872, and DeBar's Opera House, St. Louis, December 23, 1872

# GEORGE M. COHAN

c/o Cohan & Harris, Theatrical Producers
Holland Building, Broadway & 40th
New York, New York

• • • • • • • • • • • • • • • • • • • • • • • • • • • • • • • • • • • •

## SEEKING

Crackerjack talent (men & women) for chorusline roles in a series of upcoming **Musical Theatrical Extravaganzas**, both in town and on the road, to begin with the upcoming season and to continue indefinitely.

### Requirements:
☞ Women: Sing & Dance ☜
☞ Men: Sing, Dance, & Play Ball ☜

## PRODUCTIONS TO DATE

☆ **The Governor's Son**, 1901    ☆ **Running for Office**, 1903
☆ **Little Johnny Jones**, 1904    ☆ **Forty-Five Minutes from Broadway**, 1905
☆ **George Washington, Jr.**, 1906    ☆ **Fifty Miles from Boston**, 1908
☆ **The Talk of the Town**, 1907    ☆ **The American Idea**, 1908
☆ **The Yankee Prince**, 1908    ☆ **The Man Who Owns Broadway**, 1909

## ORIGINAL SONG CREDITS

✢ *If I Were Only Mr. Morgan*    ✢ *Hot Tamale Alley*
✢ *The Warmest Baby in the Bunch*    ✢ *I Guess I'll Have To Telegraph*
✢ *Give My Regards to Broadway*    *My Baby*
✢ *The Yankee Doodle Boy*    ✢ *So Long Mary*
✢ *You're a Grand Old Flag*    ✢ *Come on Down Town*

✢*Hugh McCue, You Mick*
✢*There's Something About a Uniform*
✢*Under Any Old Flag at All*
✢*When a Fellow's on the Level with a Girl That's on the Square*

## EARLY SUCCESSES

A rich, rewarding, and productive early life spent on the nationwide vaudeville circuit, beginning, as a babe in arms, with the Four Cohans, a family troupe, contributed to an unexcelled show-business education by providing firsthand experience in numerous theatrical sides including:

✪ *Human Prop* ✪ *Buck-and-Wing Dances* ✪ *Bootblack Specialties* ✪ *Irish Reels* ✪ *Fly Kid*
✪ *Sentimental Recitations* ✪ *Waltz Clogs* ✪ *Violinist* ✪ *Incorrigible Lad with a Heart of Gold*

First speaking role, *The Two Barneys*, 1887; First stagewriting contribution, *Four of a Kind*, 1889; First song published, *Why Did Nellie Leave Home?*, 1894; First significant hit song, *Venus, My Shining Love*, 1895

## NOW CASTING! PRODUCTIONS TO COMMENCE FORTHWITH!

☆ ☆ ☆

G.A.Custer.
Bt. Maj. Gen. U.S.A.

# GEORGE ARMSTRONG CUSTER

c/o Secretary of War, Department of the Interior, Washington, D.C.,
*or* Monroe & Second Streets, Monroe, Michigan

---

**Career Objective**

To obtain an authoritative leadership position that will most effectively utilize renowned, illustrious military background in an ardent endeavor to resolve the **Indian Problem** in the Western Wilderness.

**Profile**

Dynamic, effective, battle-proven Leader of Men fully capable of sound judgment, strategic planning, authoritative subordinate supervision, and glorious, heroic performance on the bloodstained field of battle. Independent, outspoken, decisive commander blind to and intolerant of cowardice and weak-willed behavior on any level; well-versed in all aspects of Indian warfare, as attested to by brilliant victory over heathen Cheyenne at the Battle of the Washita, November 1868. Stalwart, determined, and dry as a cob, he became, in 1863, the youngest Brigadier General in the history of the United States Army.

**Military Experience**

### War Between the States:
- 1862: Brigadier General, Michigan Volunteers
- 1865: Major General (Brevet)

Battles: Gettysburg, Cedarville, Brandy Station, Winchester, Yellow Tavern, Sailor's Creek, Fair Oaks, Barbee's Cross-roads, Antietam, Monterey House, Boonesboro, James City, Wilderness campaign, &c.
- Received Citation for Bravery, Battle of Bull Run
- Wounded, skirmish at Culpeper Court House, September 1863
- Present at the surrender at Appomattox Court House, April 9, 1865

### Indian Wars and Expeditions:
- Lieutenant Colonel, 7th Cavalry, 1866–Present
- Commander, Washita Campaign, Winter 1868
- Commander, Yellowstone Expedition, 1873
- Commander, Black Hills Expedition, 1874

**Education**

**Graduate**, United States Military Academy, West Point, New York, 1861
- Graduated 34th in class

**Publications**

*My Life on the Plains*, 1874

### Professional References
Available for inspection (References include Commanding General of the Army, the Secretary of War, and the President of the United States)

# Clarence Darrow

1537 East 60th Street
Chicago, Illinois

---

## DECLARATION OF INTENT

Support, advocacy, or a partnership concerning the creation, development, and advancement of a **Major League Baseball Team**, which endeavor shall fulfill the little-known lifelong ambition ("I have snatched my share of Joys from the grudging hand of fate as I have jogged along, but never has life held for me anything quite so entrancing as baseball...") of this Celebrated and Renowned Attorney, now in the Autumn of his legal career.

## BRIEF PHILOSOPHICAL DISCOURSE

A brilliant career encompassing some of the most famed and illustrious courtroom dramas of the past four decades and a personal philosophy encompassing a broad humanitarianism coupled with a sincere belief that a constructive, creative, and positive environment and means of healthy expression are of ultimate benefit to society as a whole lends credence to the proposition of personal involvement in the furthering of the Great American Pastime.

## BIOGRAPHICAL SYNOPSIS

- Born April 18, 1857, Kinsman, Ohio • Attended Allegheny College, Meadville, Pennsylvania, 1873–1874 • University of Michigan Law School, 1877 • Admitted to Ohio Bar, 1878 • Began law practice in Chicago, 1888

- **Notable cases include:**
  The Conspiracy Trial of Eugene V. Debs, Union President, 1895 • The Anthracite Coal Strike Arbitration, 1902 • Haywood, Moyer, and Pettibone Murder Defense in the Steunenberg Affair, Boise, Idaho, 1907 • *Los Angeles Times* Bombing, J. J. and J. B. McNamara, Defendants, 1911 • Leopold and Loeb Murder Trial, Chicago, 1924 • The Defense of John T. Scopes, Indicted for Teaching Evolution, Dayton, Tennessee, 1925 • The Defense of 11 Negroes Accused of the Murder of a Ku Klux Klansman, Detroit, 1926

- Additional professional positions held included Special Assessment Attorney, Corporation Counsel, and Head of the Law Department, City of Chicago; General Attorney, Chicago & North Western Railway Co.

## PUBLISHED WORKS

- *A Persian Pearl and Other Essays* (1902)
- *Farmington* (1904)
- *Russia's Message* (1908)
- *How Voltaire Fooled Priest and King* (1921)
- *Resist Not Evil* (1903)
- *Crime and Criminals* (1907)
- *An Eye for an Eye* (1914)
- *Crime: Its Cause and Treatment* (1922)

## FURTHER PARTICULARIZATIONS

Past or present member of the Henry George Single Tax Movement; the Tavern, Athletic, Press, and South Shore Country Clubs (all of Chicago); and the National Association for the Advancement of Colored People. Chief character, *Mystery of Life* (motion picture play), 1927. Retired from the Practice of Law, 1929.

# Emily Dickinson

*280 Main Street*
*Amherst, Massachusetts*

### ◌The Prospective Volition & Declaration of Intent◌

The Poetess seeks to establish contact with the Literary Public as regards the Immense body of Haunting, Mystic, & Seamless Poetry she has produced in recent years. In the estimation of her Preceptor immortality seems assured and, regardless of certain technical irregularities, the Works seem destined to place her in the Esteemed Company of the greatest American Poets.

*The thing called fame is fleet indeed*
*and trips from door to door*
*But she shall call most earnestly*
*When I am nevermore.*

### ◌Significant Persons Who Have Provided◌ Influences & Persuasions

- Benjamin F. Newton, gentle Tutor, Called Back 1853
- Henry Vaughan Emmons of Amherst College
- Rev. Dr. Charles Wadsworth, "my Shepherd"
- Samuel Bowles, Editor, *Springfield Daily Republican*
- Thomas Wentworth Higginson, Preceptor, Essayist, and Critic
- Major Edward & Mrs. Helen Hunt Jackson
- Josiah G. Holland, Editor, the *Century*
- George Gould, Union Theological Seminary

### ◌Principal Creative Inspirations◌

- John Keats
- John Ruskin
- Shakespeare
- *The Princess*
- St. John's *Revelations*

- Robert Browning
- Sir Thomas Browne
- *Evangeline*
- *The Maiden Aunt*
- *The Erlking*

### ◌Poems Published to Date◌

• "A Valentine," *Springfield Daily Republican*, February 20, 1852 • "The May-Wine," *Springfield Daily Republican*, May 4, 1861 • "My Sabbath," *The Round Table*, March 12, 1864 • "Sunset," *Springfield Daily Republican*, March 30, 1864

### ◌Formal Schooling◌

**Amherst Academy**, Amherst, Massachussets, 1847 Graduate
•Geology, Latin, Mental Philosophy, Botany
**Mount Holyoke Female Seminary**, South Hadley, Massachussetts, 1847
•Ancient History, Algebra, Ecclesiastical History, Euclid

# Isadora Duncan

*"Die Gotliche, Heilige Isadora"*

Grünewald School of Dance
Grünewald, Berlin, Germany

---

## Avocational Ambition

An opportunity to elevate the popular conception of Modern Interpretive Dance in America to the status of creative and original art.

## Profile of Professional Rôle

Revolutionary artist possessed both of ideas and conceptions much in advance of their time and of lofty, ethereal talents emanating from the center of the Real World of ideal Love, Beauty, and Art. Dedicated and devoted to evolving interpretive dance into a medium of expression as has hitherto found utterance in music and literature. Important influences include Walt Whitman, Nietzsche, and the Greeks as well as (as related to Art & Expression) the works of Brahms, Wagner, Beethoven, Tschaikowsky, and Chopin.

*On with the Dance! Let joy be unconfin'd;*
*No sleep till morn, when Youth and Pleasure meet*
*To chase the glowing Hours with flying feet.*

—Byron, *Childe Harold, III*

## Biographical Narration & Accomplishments

✦ Born in San Francisco, California, May 27, 1878, of the poet Joseph Charles Duncan and Dora Gray, musician; three siblings.

✦ **Education:** Irrelevant & immaterial, with the exception of the tutelage of the poetess Ina Donna Coolbrith, Librarian, Oakland Public Library. Began teaching dance at the age of six; abandoned drab, dismal public education in 1888 and opened, with sister Elizabeth, a school teaching the "new system" of dance.

✦ **Early Performances Include:**
  • Augusta Duncan's San Francisco Barn Theatre, 1890
  • Roof Garden Theatre, Chicago, 1894–1895
  • Augustin Daly's Theatrical Company, New York, 1896–1898
    (Appeared in theatrical production of *A Midsummer Night's Dream*, 1898)

✦ **European Travels & Successes:**
  • Intensive study of Greek Art, British Museum, London, 1899
  • Private performances culminating in debut at New Gallery, London, 1900
    (Charles Hallé, Artist/Director)
  • Dance Company of Loie Fuller, Vienna, 1902
  • Solo Tour, Budapest, Vienna, Munich, and Berlin, 1902–1903
  • Created "Temple of the Dance", Athens, 1904
  • Founded Grünewald School of Dance, 1904
  • Russian Tours, 1905 and 1907–1908

## Colleagues & Associates

✦ Alexander Grosz, Impresario, Munich ✦ Cosima Wagner, widow of the composer, Bayreuth, Germany
✦ Mrs. Patrick Campbell, London ✦ Sergey Diaghilev, Moscow

MISS DUNCAN INTENDS TO EMBARK ON AN AMERICAN TOUR THIS SUMMER

# Amelia Earhart

c/o G. P. Putnam Estate, Rye, New York
or, Bureau of Air Commerce
Department of Commerce, State Department
Washington, D.C.

## Notice of Intent to Secure the
## Services of a Qualified Aeronautical Navigator

Seeking to enlist an experienced Celestial/Radio Navigator to join in a proposed around-the-world flight to be piloted and commanded by the renowned aviatrix.

## Outline of Flight Plan

An East-to-West equatorial flight originating in Oakland, California. The route as planned at this time will include the Hawaiian Islands; Howland Island in the Central Pacific; Lae, New Guinea; Darwin, Australia; Singapore; Calcutta; then through the Middle East to the east coast of Africa; across Africa through Khartoum to Dakar; across the South Atlantic to Fortaleza, Brazil; northwest along the South American coast to Puerto Rico and Florida; and thence cross-country to terminate in Oakland.

## The Aircraft and Equipment

✛ Lockheed Electra 10E (NR 16020) ✛
✛ Twin Pratt & Whitney Wasp engines (1100 total horsepower) ✛
✛ Constant speed propellers ✛
✛ 1,202-gallon fuel capacity (maximum range 4,500 miles) ✛
✛ Radio Direction Finders and Sperry Robot Pilot ✛
✛ Bendix Loop Antennae ✛

## Brief History of Pilot's Aeronautical Accomplishments

- First woman to cross the Atlantic by air (as logkeeper) in the Fokker Tri-motor *Friendship*, William L. "Bill" Stultz, pilot, June 1928
- Set altitude record for autogyros (18,415 feet) in a Pitcairn Autogyro, 1931
- Solo Atlantic flight, May 20–21, 1932 (Lockheed Vega)
- Set women's transcontinental speed record, August 24–25, 1932 (established new record July 7–8, 1933)
- First pilot to solo across the Pacific (Honolulu–San Francisco), January 1935

## Related Information

- Received flight instruction from Anita "Neta" Snook, first female graduate of the Curtiss School of Aviation
- Soloed June 1921 in a Kinner Airster and set women's altitude record of 14,000 feet
- First President of the Ninety-Nines (women pilots' organization), 1929–1933
- Awarded Gold Aviation Medal, National Geographic Society, 1932
- Employed as: Public Relations Consultant, Transcontinental Air Transport; Aviation Editor, *Cosmopolitan* magazine; Vice-President, Ludington Airlines

INTERESTED PARTIES CONTACT MISS EARHART OR GEORGE P. PUTNAM THROUGH THE ABOVE ADDRESS
—OR—
THE PUBLISHING FIRM OF G. P. PUTNAM'S SONS, NEW YORK

# Wyatt Berry Stapp Earp
c/o W. W. "Whitey" Rupp's Keno House
Main Street & Douglas Avenue
Wichita, Kansas

## Nature of Proposal

In response to repeated urgent inquiries sent by post and wire from Mayor George Hoover of Dodge City, the addressor announces his willingness to accept the post of Chief Deputy Marshall, at the agreed salary of $250 per month and found, as well as additamentary remunerations amounting to $2.50 for every arrest carried into effect.

## Particularization of Pertinent Attributes

- Proven man of action and hard-edged determination; sober, resolute, & forthright—**never** known to show the white feather under any circumstances, heeled or otherwise.
- Renowned throughout the buffalo range, the Indian Nations, and the entire Western Frontier as a Paladin of unexcelled fearlessness, manly prowess, and bull-dog courage.
- Very well versed in the pugilistic arts; gun-throwing skills with rifle, shotgun, & pistol are of the highest order; originator & master of the "buffaloing" technique of temporary incapacitation.

## Representative Instances of Law Enforcement Proficiencies

▶ Pulled in Ben Thompson's horns, Ellsworth, Kansas, August 1873

▶ Put a head on Shanghai Pierce and studded his bunch of Texas cow-boys before they hurrahed Wichita, June 1874

▶ Yerked & whipped George Peshaur, bare-knuckled, at Dick Cogswell's cigar store, Wichita, July 1874

▶ Run it over for Mannen Clements and his 40 Texas men on the Douglas Avenue roadway as they set out to tree the town, August 1874, Wichita

▶ Ran down and recovered 1,600 longhorns rustled from George Ulrich's outfit by the McMurray-Anderson gang, Wewoka Valley, Indian Nations, November 1874

▶ Bluffed & buffaloed Sergeant King, Army bad man, July 1875, Wichita

## Earlier Lines of Work

- **Hunter**, Government Surveying Party, Indian Nations, December 1869–April 1871 ($35 per month in addition to 10 cents per pound for buffalo meat, $1 per deer or antelope, $1.50 per wild turkey)
- **Buffalo Hunter**, three seasons, 1871–1874
- **Freighting Partner** (w/Charles Chrisman), Salt Lake–Julesburg Trail, 1867
- **16-Mule-Team Driver**, Chris Taylor Co., San Bernardino–Salt Lake, 1866
- **10-Mule-Team Driver** (Frank Binkley, Boss), San Pedro–Prescott line, 1866

TESTIMONIALS AVAILABLE FROM NUMEROUS LEADING CITIZENS AT TRAILHEAD TOWNS THROUGHOUT KANSAS, AS WELL AS FROM THE UNION PACIFIC RAILROAD, OMAHA

# Frances Farmer

c/o Knickerbocker Hotel
Hollywood, California

## Professional Goals

The actress wishes to explore and secure serious professional stage roles that will effectively expose and utilize her unique and proven thespian talents. Motion picture offers will be carefully reviewed, but it must be understood that no frivolous, fatuous, shallow, or "blonde" roles will be considered.

## Stage, Screen, and Radio Credits

### Stage:

→ Clifford Odets' *Golden Boy*     Group Theatre     New York & On Tour
→ Irwin Shaw's *Quiet City*     Broadway
→ *At Mrs. Beams*     Westchester Playhouse
→ *Thunder Rock*     Group Theatre     New York

### Film Work:

| Film Work: | Role: | Director: |
|---|---|---|
| → *Among the Living* w/Susan Hayward | Featured | Heisler |
| → *Badlands of Dakota* | Calamity Jane | Green |
| → *World Premiere* w/John Barrymore | Featured | Tetzlaff |
| → *Flowing Gold* w/John Garfield | Featured | Green |
| → *South of Pago Pago* | Featured | Green |
| → *Ride a Crooked Mile* | Featured | Green |
| → *Ebb Tide* | Faith Wishart | Hogan |
| → *The Toast of New York* w/Cary Grant | Josie Mansfield | Lee |
| → *Exclusive* | Featured | Hall |
| → *Come and Get It* | Lotta Bostrom | Hawks & Wyler |
| → *Rhythm on the Range* w/Bing Crosby | Featured | Taurog |
| → *Border Flight* | Featured | Lovering |
| → *Too Many Parents* | Featured | McGowan |

### Radio:

→ Lux Radio Theatre, *Men in White* w/Spencer Tracy, 1937
→ Lux Radio Theatre, *British Agent* w/Errol Flynn, 1937

## Education/Training

Drama/Journalism Major, University of Washington, Seattle, Washington
  • Role of Else Brandt in student production of Sidney Howard's *Alien Corn*
  • Won $100 and trip to Russia in essay contest, 1934

## Specialized Talents

• Various Accents and Inflections • The Stanislavsky Method • Piano
• Poetry • Swimming

# Stephen C. Foster

Griffin Boardinghouse
421 East 4th Street
Cincinnati, Ohio

Peters, Field, & Co.
12th & Walnut Street
Cincinnati, Ohio

## ♪ PROCLAMATION OF INTENT ♪

To secure popular publication of the most recent specimens of songs and ballads currently being produced by the Gentleman and to establish a relationship with reputable music publishers that will serve to be mutually beneficial by virtue of a contractual agreement based solely on royalty payments.

## ♪ DELINEATION ♪

A rare and lofty musical talent readily discernible at an early age and encouraged by his mother (who presented him, at age seven, with a flageolet that he mastered immediately) has coalesced into the prodigious output of ingenuous melodies of homely simplicity and tenderness as well as numerous Ethiopian ditties possessed of a distinctive unpretentiousness of musical idiom and style. All indications are that these unique and beautiful vocalisms will enter into the mainstream of the culture and prove to be of lasting quality.

## ♪ SONGS PUBLISHED TO DATE ♪

*There's a Good Time Coming* –1846

*Lou'siana Belle* –1847

*What Must a Fairy's Dream Be?* –1847

*Uncle Ned* –1848

*Stay Summer Breath* –1848

*Away Down South* –1848

*Oh, Susanna* –1848

(Note: This particular melody may prove in time to be of special merit and interest.
It has been generally accepted as the leitmotif of the Great California Gold Rush.
Furthermore, European agents report a rendition currently popular on the streets of Berlin,
viz: "Ich Komm von Alabama, Mit der Banjo auf dem Knie."

*Dolly Jones* –1849

*Summer Longings* –1849

*Nelly Was a Lady* –1849

*My Brudder Gum* –1849

## ♪ WORKS IN PROGRESS ♪

• A merry and nimble Ethiopian ditty based on the ribald revelry common to the Camptown racetrack. Being composed for the minstrel circuit.

• A touching and sentimental ballad inspired by a prodigal's longing to return to his home on the Peedee River. A more euphonious name for the river may be selected before the song is published, however.

## ♪ EARLY LIFE ♪

Studied at Athens Academy, Tioga Point, Pennsylvania, where first musical effort, *Tioga Waltz*, was presented, 1841 • Attended Jefferson College, Canonsburg, for a period of five days. Complete lack of interest in academic pursuits, excessive daydreaming, and uncontrollable inclination to pursue all things musical led to an early end of college career • First song, *Open Thy Lattice, Love*, published 1841 • Member, Knights of the S.T.—Motto: "Heroes, Fail Not"

*References available from Thomas "Daddy" Rice, The Sable Harmonists, & E. P. Christy*

# Marcus Moziah Garvey, D.C.L.

114 West 138th Street
Harlem, New York City, New York

## Supreme Purpose

To establish an autonomous African State dedicated to the furthering of the causes of Negro peoples worldwide, which State will embody all-Negro government, systems of trade and educational institutions, and a Black Deity.

## Descriptive Profile Narration

Self-made leader ardently dedicated to drawing all people of the Negro race together with the ultimate design of absolute self-sufficiency in matters of government, economics, religion, education, and trade. Fiery orator and organizer possessing refined journalistic and communications skills that facilitate effective expression of ideas concerning racial equality and independence.

## Chronicle of Relevant Information

### Education:

- St. Ann's Bay Elementary School, St. Ann's Bay, Jamaica
- Queen of England High School, St. Ann's Bay
- Tutorial edifications administered by Reverend W. H. Sloely and Reverend P. A. Conahan
- Birbeck College, London, England

### Employment:

- Apprentice to Mr. Burrowes, Printer, St. Ann's Bay, 1901
- Master Printer/Foreman, P. A. Benjamin Co., Kingston, Jamaica, 1906
- Timekeeper, United Fruit Company, Costa Rica, 1907

### Publications:

- ➤ Editor, *Garvey's Watchman*, Jamaica
- ➤ Editor, *Our Own*, Jamaica
- ➤ Publisher/Editor, *La Nacionale*, Port Limón, Panama
- ➤ Publisher/Editor, *La Prensa*, Colón, Panama
- ➤ Writer, *Africa Times* and *Orient Review*, London, England
- ➤ Publisher, *Negro World*, New York City (circulation in excess of 50,000 within one year)

### Organizations:

- Founder **Universal Negro Improvement and Conservation Association and African Communities League**, 1914
  —The stated purpose of the organization is to establish a Universal Confraternity among the race, to promote the spirit of race pride and love, to reclaim the fallen of the race, and to assist in civilizing the backward tribes of Africa.
- Founder **Black Star Steamship Line** and **Negro Factories Corporation**

### *Reference:*

*Duse Mohammed Ali, London, England/Cairo, Egypt*

# GERONIMO
## (Go-yah-kla)
c/o Commanding Officer, Fort Sill
Lawton, Oklahoma Territory

## STATEMENT OF INTENT & PURPOSE

To petition the President of the United States, the War Department, and all the citizens of the nation as regards the following matters:

1. The current situation of the displaced Apache prisoners of war and their desire to return to their ancestral homelands in the Southwest.
2. Official sanction & permission to publish the story of the life of the great leader Geronimo, with the guarantee that such publication will not unfavorably affect the aforementioned Apache prisoners.

## BRIEF BIOGRAPHICAL DISCOURSE

The renowned warrior-leader was born into the Bedonkohe band of the Apache nearly 80 years ago at No-doyohn Cañon in present-day Arizona Territory, the fourth of eight children of the extended family of Taklishim and Juana. Exposure to traditional & ancient Apache lore, legend, saga, and allegory with its pronounced emphasis on the relationship of his people to their natural enemies as well as the extreme significance & importance of residing in divinely ordained homelands resulted in evolution into a warrior-chieftain of the highest order. These factors must be considered when attempting to understand the current motivations of the Apache people, as well as the conflicts of the past 50 years.

## MEXICAN RAIDS & DEPREDATIONS

➤ 1859: Arizpe, Sonora, in revenge for the massacre at Kas-ki-yeh (Janos)
➤ 1859: Sierra de Antunez, with Ah-koch-ne and Ko-deh-ne, warriors
➤ 1860: Sierra de Sahuaripa, battle with Mexican cavalry (injured)
➤ 1861: Casa Grande, Chihuahua, pack train captured
➤ 1862: Sierra Madre and Sierra de Sahuaripa, pack trains captured
➤ 1863–1867: Crassanas and Pontoco, Sonora; Yaqui River; Casa Grande; Santa Cruz, Sonora; Arizpe; Sierra de Sahuaripa

## BRIEF & PERFUNCTORY HISTORIETTE

● **Participant** in the action at Apache Pass against General Carleton's forces, July, 1862 ● **Battles** with Mexican troops, 1867; 1873–1880; 1883–1884 ● **Skirmish** with 6th U.S. Cavalry, 1881 ● **Battle** with forces of Lt. Col. Forsyth, 1882 ● **Clash** with Mexican troops of Col. Lorenzo Garcia, 1882 ● **Surrendered** to: Apache Agent John P. Clum, 1877; General Willcox, 1880; General Crook, 1883 & 1886; General Miles, 1886 ● **Escaped** from San Carlos reservation: 1876, 1878, 1881, 1885 ● **Transported** as prisoner to Ft. Pickens, Florida, 1886 ● **Transferred** to Ft. Sill, 1894

## RECOMMENDATIONS & SUBSTANTIATIONS

◆ S. M. Barrett, Superintendent of Education, Lawton, O.T. ◆ Dr. J. M. Greenwood, Superintendent of Schools, Kansas City, Missouri ◆ Major Charles Taylor, Ft. Sill, O.T. ◆ David R. Boyd, President, University of Oklahoma

# Jay Gould

**33 East 17th Street**
**New York, New York**

---

**Purpose** To prevail upon the New York State Legislature to immediately enact favorable legislation, *ex post facto*, which will enable, solely with the best interests of the General Public in mind, the directorate of the Erie Railroad to issue for sale stock and convertible bonds at their discretion, to break the corner that mariner from Staten Island is attempting to place on Erie stock, and to open discreet avenues of communication with various State Representatives concerning very bountiful proposed pecuniary endowments to the General Fund.

**Delineation** Hard-edged, no-nonsense, resolute Financier currently associated in various endeavors with other like-minded capitalists in a Triumvirate intent on expanding the reaches of the Railroads ever deeper into the Western Wilderness. Untroubled by bothersome scruples or a moral need to justify individual proprietorship of enormous wealth; proven history of executing shrewd, sagacious, and Napoleonic business dealings, which substantiates a reputation for an uncanny ability to accumulate excessive amounts of capital.

**Railroad Ventures**
Directorate, 1867–Present (with James Fisk and Daniel Drew)
**Erie Railroad**
President/Secretary/Treasurer/Line Superintendent, 1863
**Rutland & Washington Railroad**
Manager, 1863
**Rensselaer & Saratoga Railway**

*Thimble Rigging, Stock & Bond Juggling, and Strategic Betrayals:*
● Atlantic & Great Western Railway
● Pittsburgh, Fort Wayne & Chicago R.R.
● Michigan Southern & Northern Indiana R.R.
● Cleveland & Pittsburgh R.R.
● Rutland & Washington R.R.
● Boston, Hartford & Erie R.R.
● Philadelphia & Erie R.R.
● Pennsylvania R.R.

**Further Enterprises**
Leather Merchant, 39 Spruce Street, New York, 1860
Partner, Smith, Gould & Martin, Wall Street, 1861
Partner, Gould, Leupp & Lee, New York, 1857
Partner (w/Zadock Pratt), Gould & Pratt Tannery, Gouldsville/Prattsville,
Pennsylvania, 1857–1858
Mapmaker/Surveyor, 1854–1857
    Ulster, Albany, Delaware Counties, New York
    Lake & Geauga Counties, Ohio
    Oakland County, Michigan
    Projected R.R. line between Newburgh & Syracuse, New York
Inventor, A Better Mousetrap, 1853

**Publication** *History of Delaware County and the Border Wars of New York, Containing a Sketch of the Early Settlement of the County and a History of the Late Anti-Rent Difficulties, with Other Historical and Miscellaneous Matter Never Before Published*, 1856

# WOODY GUTHRIE
### (WOODROW WILSON BY GOD GUTHRIE)
### ALMANAC HOUSE
### 130 WEST 10TH STREET
### N.Y., NEW YORK TOWN, N.Y., NEW YORK, N.Y., N.Y.C., NEW YORK

## Intent, Plan, & Employment Objective
Lookin' for a job with honest pay.

## Short-Winded Particularization
Mediumly well-known ballad songmaker and singer as well as great historical bum and lone-some traveler with many a hungry mile spent ramblin' down that long and mighty hard road; world citizen, migrant working man, and boomchasin' Dust Bowl refugee carrying an ever-ready, hard-hittin,' fascist-killing gitbox. Double toughest trouble buster on the shantyirons and creator of a whole stable of songs and ballads guaranteed to keep the big bosses, rich politicians, cops, scabs, and gun thugs mighty jumpy, songs of the people and the Unions, songs that have fought a million battles and never lost a-one, migratious songs that have their roots & origins dead-set center on the pulse of the Nation, songs that turn the darkness to dawn, eternal songs free for the askin', leaping, caterwaulin', hollerin' songs, songs that make folks feel good about themselves, and that...well, that's about the biggest thing that man has ever done.

## Some Songs Already Wrote Up and Written Down
▶ Union Maid
▶ Tom Joad
▶ So Long, It's Been Good to Know You
▶ They Laid Jesus Christ in His Grave
▶ Dust Bowl Refugee
▶ California Blues
▶ Roll on Columbia
▶ Do-Re-Mi
▶ I Ain't Got No Home
▶ Lonesome Valley
▶ Pretty Boy Floyd
▶ Worried Man Blues

## Ramblings, Travels, Occupations, & Other Pursuits
✪ Born and raised up in Okemah, Oklahoma; first hit the road for the Texas Gulf Coast long about 1928; settled in Pampa for a spell ✪ Camped & tramped the cinder dumps & rode the blinds and rods on the flatwheelers, deadenders, and fast rattlers on the big lines, mains, stems, and spurs to a thousand towns and worked a thousand jobs in the wheatfields & lumber camps & mills & oil towns & fruit fields; played guitar and harmonica for a living here & there and met every color and kind of a human being you can imagine ✪ Rolled into New York town some time back and that's the way she sits now, here in this good year of Nineteen and Forty-One ✪

## Musical Endeavors and Suchlike Truck
• String Band, Pampa, Texas, 1931 • First collection of songs, 1935 • Singer/Guitarist, "Woody and Lefty Lou," KFVD–Los Angeles & XELO–Tijuana, 1937–1939 • Song collection, *On a Slow Train Through California*, 1939 • Daily columnist, "Woody Sez", **People's Daily World** and **Daily Worker** • Member, Almanac Singers • *Dust Bowl Ballads*, RCA Victor, 1940 • *Library of Congress Recordings* (w/Alan Lomax), 1940 • *Cavalcade of America* (CBS) • *Back Where I Come From* (CBS) • *Folk Songs of America* (w/Leadbelly) • Benefit performances include shows for the Spanish Refugee Relief Fund & Abe Lincoln Brigade •

"THIS OLE WORLD'S IN A BAD CONDITION, BUT A NEW ONE'S IN THE MAIL."

# JOE HILL
## (or, Joseph Hillstrom)
Joe Hill Defense Committee
c/o William D. Haywood & Elizabeth Gurley Flynn
Industrial Workers of the World Headquarters
1001 West Madison Street, Chicago, Illinois

---

### PURPOSE & INTENT

To continue and nurture National and Worldwide protest regarding the *False Accusations* and *Miscarriage of Justice* surrounding the current *Kangaroo Court Proceedings* as concerns the *Malevolent & Wrongful Persecution* on first-degree murder charges of Fellow Worker Joe Hill, IWW Songwriter, by the State of Utah, William Spry, Governor.

### A BRIEF BIOGRAPHICAL DELINEATION

☞ Born Joel Hägglund, October 7, 1879, in Gävle, Sweden; emigrated to the United States in 1902
☞ Joined IWW in San Pedro, California, 1910
☞ Migrant Worker throughout the West, 1902–1914, including:
  • Construction Worker • Pipefitter • Wheat Harvester • Longshoreman
  • Lumberjack, Snohomish Lumber Co., Everett, Washington
  • Machinist, Silver King Mines, Park City, Utah
  • Hard Rock Miner, Bingham Canyon Copper Mines
  • Common Seaman, the *Sarah Cleghorn*, out of Victoria, B.C.

The **Defense Committee** contends that the *Unconstitutional Prosecution* of Fellow Worker Hill originates in not only his fervent support of the **IWW Cause** but as a result of his writing **Stirring and Inflammatory** songs in support of the Movement. Included are:

✗ *There Is a Power in a Union*    ✗ *Workers of the World Awaken*
✗ *The White Slave*    ✗ *Where the Fraser River Flows*
✗ *Casey Jones, the Union Scab*    ✗ *Mr. Block*
✗ *The Preacher and the Slave*    ✗ *Rebel Girl* (Written in jail
✗ *The Tramp*      in May of this year)

### THE FACTS CONCERNING THE CRIME

1. Grocer J. G. Morrison and son murdered by two assailants in his Salt Lake City store, 1/10/14. An ex-policeman, he had often expressed fear of retaliation from criminals he had arrested, and had recently mentioned two by name.
2. The full extent of Joe Hill's criminal record is a 30-day vagrancy jolt in San Pedro.
3. NO positive eyewitness identification, NO motive, NO gun, NO bullet.
4. One of the gunmen was wounded in the attack, and Fellow Worker Hill was treated for a gunshot wound on the evening of the 10th. Four other gunshot-wound cases were reported in Salt Lake City that night, but *none* were investigated.
5. Joe Hill tried and convicted by the capitalist-inspired Court of Public Hysteria on June 26, 1914; death sentence passed July 8.

### POPULAR SUPPORT & APPEALS FOR CLEMENCY

Thousands of communications protesting the sentence have been sent to the Governor of Utah from around the globe, including appeals from Samuel Gompers, Helen Keller, Eugene V. Debs, W. A. F. Ekengren (Swedish Ambassador), and a direct appeal to Governor Spry from President Wilson.

*"He's in their dungeon, dark and grim*
*He stood by us, we'll stand by him."*

# Billie Holiday

*286 West 142nd Street*
*New York, New York*

## Plan, Purpose, and Intention

*To open a long-term gig at Barney Josephson's new Café Society in Greenwich Village, an innovative and socially progressive club modeled after the traditional European cabarets.*

## Artistic Profile & Delineation

*A nonpareil style characterized by qualities of graceful phrasing and uncommonly delicate timbre as well as a pronounced capacity to lyricize in a distinctive, instrumentally influenced fashion combines with rare powers of rhythmic and melodic expression to produce, with unparalleled elements of majesty, mood, wit, and emotion, a timeless jazz vocal delivery of a unique and higher order. Lady Day's style is firmly rooted in the blues tradition, although in an emotional rather than technical sense, and conveys, with sublime and astonishing accuracy and perfection, the greatest heights of elation and deepest pits of despair that characterize the true state of the human condition.*

## Partial Listing of New York Club Gigs, 1930–Present

- *Grey Dawn (Brooklyn)*
- *Clark Monroe's (134th Street)*
- *Dickie Wells' Clam House*
- *Ubangi Club*
- *Hot Cha Club*
- *Mexico's*
- *Pod's & Jerry's Log Cabin*

- *Alhambra Grill*
- *Goldgraben's*
- *Monette's*
- *Yeah Man Club*
- *Big John's Café*
- *Shim Sham Club*
- *The Apollo Theatre*

## New Works Being Prepared for Presentation

➤ *A poignant, sentimental, and touching ballad extolling the merits of the self-made individual. The overall theme of the piece is one of self-sufficiency, and work on the lyrics is in progress at the present time: "God helps the child who helps himself."*

➤ *A haunting, disturbing, and politically significant song, hard and angry, meant to raise the public consciousness regarding the barbaric state of race relations in the South. Being composed in the key of B-flat minor, a traditional key well suited for more dolorous and somber compositions.*

## Representative Repertoire

*• I Must Have That Man • Fine and Mellow • Miss Brown to You • Riffin' the Scotch • It's Too Hot for Words • Them There Eyes • Your Mother's Son-in-Law • Why Was I Born? • Billie's Blues • Swing, Brother, Swing • I Cried for You • I Wished on the Moon • This Year's Kisses • Summertime • The Man I Love • Me, Myself and I • Trav'lin' All Alone • I'll Get By*

## Testimonials & Recommendations Available From:

♪ *Count Basie* ♪ *Artie Shaw* ♪ *Benny Goodman* ♪ *Lester Young* ♪ *Joe Glaser* ♪ *John Hammond* ♪

*Significant Influences Include Louis Armstrong and Bessie Smith*

# Harry Houdini

394 East 21st Street
Flatbush, Brooklyn, New York

## Purpose and Intent

To expose and discredit all purveyors of fraud, trickery, and deceit as concerns mediums, seances, "spirit mediums, and the like, as well as humbug practitioners of conjuring, magic, and escapology."

*"The Handcuff King & Monarch of Leg Shackles"*
or
*"The Elusive American"*
is renowned on the Continent & in America as
*"The Greatest Mystifier That History Chronicles"*

## Conjurations & Illusions

- Regulation Double Lock Tower Leg-Irons
- The Extraordinary Bean Giant
- Maltby Dead Lock Shackles
- East Indian Needle Trick
- De Kolta's Marvelous Cube
- French Thumb-Screw
- The Bottle Neck
- Imperator Irons
- German Transport Chain
- Crystal Casket
- Vanishing Elephant

## Authorships & Publications

- *The Unmasking of Robert-Houdin,* 1908
- *The Right Way to Do Wrong—An Unmasking of Successful Criminals*
- *The Adventurous Life of a Versatile Artist*
- *America's Sensational Perplexer*
- Publisher, "The Conjurer's Monthly", 1906–1908

## Fraternities & Associations

President, Society of American Magicians
Member, Magician's Club of London
Member, Pastime Athletic Club, New York

## Notable Engagements

- ★ Tony Pastor's Theatre (New York)
- ★ Hammerstein's Roof Garden (New York)
- ★ Orpheum Circuit
- ★ Alhambra Theatre

And a Sensational, Seemingly Impossible Escape Performed in Full View of an Incredulous & Astonished Audience at Scotland Yard! (Word sent to the Queen).

# Anna M. Jarvis

East Main Street ♥ Grafton, West Virginia

---

## Pronouncement of Intent

To establish a national holiday in the Spring of the year
that will, in the manner of the Mothering Sunday observed during
Lent in Medieval England, honor, recognize, and cherish the
Institution of American Motherhood.

## Syllabus of Personal Philosophy

Proper and upright spinster possessing staunch and deep-rooted convictions concerning the
sacred status of the American family (struggling, as it is, with the hectic pace of modern life)
as well as the implicit belief that no greater tragedy can befall a Christian than to fail to
cherish and honor a Mother, with all due filial love and devotion, before it is too late.

## Historiette, and Compendium of Successes on Behalf of the Establishment of the Holiday

- ♥ Born May 1, 1864, Webster, West Virginia; raised in Grafton
- ♥ Graduate of the Female Seminary, Wheeling, West Virginia
- ♥ Mother, Anna Reese Jarvis, Sunday School Teacher at Andrews Methodist Church for 20 years, departed this mortal coil May 9, 1905
- ♥ Miss Jarvis institutes strenuous, energetic, and tireless letter-writing campaign to myriad Clergymen, Senators, Publishers, Congressmen, Evangelists, Titans of Business, Governors, and other Stalwarts of Society on behalf of the Campaign, 1908.
- ♥ In 1910 West Virginia and Oklahoma proclaim official Mother's Day holiday; Washington State soon follows; within the year all States of the Union do likewise.
- ♥ Organized International Mother's Day Association, December 1912
- ♥ Appointed Delegate to 7th World's Sunday School Convention, Zurich, 1913

*"It is the day of all the year*
*Of all the year the one day*
*When I shall see my mother dear*
*And bring her cheer,*
*A-mothering on Sunday."*

—George Hare Leonard

## Supporters & Followers

• John Wanamaker of Philadelphia • Senators Heflin of Alabama & Sheppard of Texas
• Governor Hay of Washington • Wilbur Chapman, Evangelist

# Jack Johnson

c/o Jack Johnson's Main Event Café
Tijuana, Baja California, Mexico

—or—

3344 Wabash Avenue
Chicago, Illinois

## Notice of Petition

The former Heavyweight Champion of the World respectfully announces his intention to surrender to the proper authorities at a specified location on the U.S.–Mexican border and thereby to be transported to Chicago to answer federal charges resulting from his conviction on May 13, 1913 as a result of an indictment handed down in the court of Judge Kennesaw Mountain Landis regarding alleged violations of the Mann Act of 1910.

## Bio-Scape of Athletic Prowess, Notoriety, & Renown

Acclaimed by many pugilistic pundits as the greatest heavyweight, regardless of race or creed, the manly sport has yet seen, "Li'l Arthur," or "The Black Fire," or "Big Smoke," as he has been affectionately or otherwise called, rode to stellar heights of international fame as a result of the universal recognition of his peerless and unparalleled fisticuffical finesse, the blinding speed of his blows, and the thunderous, pile-driving powers of devastation displayed in the ring as well as his bold, unconventional, assertive, and somewhat audacious personal codes of conduct, rather blatant disregard for certain accepted social and interpersonal standards of behavior, and his proven fortitude in meeting the challenge of the resultant wave of vituperative, poisonous, and insane public sentiment as displayed by a sizeable percentage of the Caucasian-American populace.

## Chronology of Fistic History, Bouts, & Matches

- Came up on the road and on the Galveston, Texas, docks; pugilistic education was furthered in sideshow rings, amateur bouts, and by victories in numerous "Battle Royal" matches presented as stag parties at the Royal Sporting Club, Galveston.

- Partial listing of combats & contests includes:

    • K.O.'D JIM "THE GALVESTON GIANT" MCCORMICK, FEBRUARY 1899 • LOST TO KLONDIKE JOHN HAYNES, MAY 1899 • WHIPPED BY JOE "THE GRADUATE PROFESSOR" CHOYNSKI, FEBRUARY 1901

    • K.O.'D JACK "THE OTHER" JEFFRIES IN 5, MAY 1902 • LICKED MEXICAN PETE EVERETT, SEPTEMBER 1902 • BEAT DENVER ED MARTIN IN 20, FEBRUARY 1903 • K.O.'D JIM JEFFORDS AND BLACK BILL IN BOUTS A WEEK APART, 1905 • BEAT SAM "THE BOSTON TAR BABY" LANGFORD, APRIL 1906 • WHIPPED SAILOR BURKE, SEPTEMBER 1907 • K.O.'D FIREMAN JIM FLYNN IN 11, NOVEMBER 1907 • 9 MATCHES WITH JOE JEANNETTE, 1905–1908

    **Knocked out Tommy Burns in 14 rounds for the Heavyweight Championship of the World, Rushcutter's Bay, Australia, December 26, 1908, Hugh D. "Huge Deal" McIntosh, Promoter**

- 10 TITLE DEFENSES, 1910–1914, INCLUDING 15-ROUND K.O. OF JIM JEFFRIES IN RENO, NEVADA, JULY 4, 1910 • DETHRONED BY JESS WILLARD, HAVANA, CUBA, APRIL 5, 1915 (26 ROUNDS)

<u>Overall Record: 70-6-12</u>

## Notable Acquaintances & Advocates with Whom Associated
## During Exile & Expatriation, 1913-Present

• Nicholas II, Last Tsar of Russia • Grigori Efimovitch Rasputin • Raymond Poincaré, President of France • Kaiser Wilhelm of Germany • Mata Hari • Venustiano Carranza, late President of Mexico • Manuel II, deposed King of Portugal • Joselito and Belmonte, Kings of Spanish Matadors • General Mario G. Menocal, President of Cuba

"LIKE ME, YOU WILL BE IMPERISHABLE IN HISTORY." —Grigori Rasputin

# Scott Joplin

### Roasalline Boarding House, West 29th Street
### New York, New York

---

## Proposed Endeavor

Publication and Production of the Grand Opera *Treemonisha*, the primary obstacle to which is the indisputable fact that the Masterwork is generations ahead of its time, but which ultimate presentation on the stage to the American Public shall fulfill the lifelong ambition of the Illustrious & Storied **King of Ragtime Music**.

## Concise Abstract of the Opus

❖ The Composer wishes it clearly understood that ***Treemonisha***, while employing a syncopated style, is not ragtime, with its roots in Jump Jim Crow, Jig-Time, and Zip Coon, but rather an opera in the grand tradition, albeit uniquely American.

❖ The work is the culmination of 15 years' labor, completed in September of this year; 3 acts, 11 characters, chorus, 27 musical pieces, 230 pages of score.

❖ The theme of the opera is a celebration of Afro-American culture, and explores the Composer's conviction that the status of the Negro people in this country shall be elevated only by virtue of education & enlightenment and the casting off of the platitudinous fallacies, Stygian ignorance, and voodoo superstitions that have historically hindered the social progress and melioration of the Ethiopian race.

## Brief Sum & Substance of the Story-Line

The opera begins in September 1884 on an antebellum plantation near the town of Texarkana, close by the Red River in Arkansas. Eighteen years previous Ned and Monisha, a childless couple living on the plantation, found a two-day-old baby girl under a tree and claimed her as their own. Determined that the child not be raised in ignorance and superstition, an agreement is reached with a neighboring white woman to provide her with an education. Now grown to a proud, confident, and enlightened young woman, Treemonisha endeavors to lead her people to a luminous new future embracing education, progress, and truth.

## Prior Music Publishers Who Will Provide References

♦ John Stark & Son, St. Louis & Sedalia, Missouri ♦ Stark Music Co., New York & St. Louis ♦ Jos. W. Stern & Co., New York ♦ Seminary Music Company, New York ♦ Val. A. Reis Music Company, St. Louis ♦ Robert Smith, Temple, Texas ♦ Success Music Co., Chicago ♦ Thiebes–Stierlin Music Co., St. Louis

## Early Life and Musical Development

♦ First musical training under tutelage of Julius Weiss, Texarkana
♦ Student, Lincoln High School, Sedalia, Missouri
♦ Arrangement, Harmony, & Composition Studies, George R. Smith College for Negroes, Sedalia
♦ Accompanist, Texas Medley Quartet
♦ Pianist, "Honest John's" Silver Dollar Saloon, St. Louis
♦ Jig Pianist, World's Columbian Exposition, Chicago, 1893
♦ 50+ ragtime songs published, 1895–Present

**Member, Colored Vaudeville Benevolent Association**

### David Laamea Kamanakaupuu Mahinulani Naloiaehuokalaii Lumialani
# Kalakaua
*(or "Taffy," as he is known within a close circle of intimates)*
c/o Iolani Palace, Bishop Street
Honolulu, Kingdom of Hawaii

---

## Statement of Intent
To restore and preserve the Ancient Order of Hawaii with all Traditional Customs Intact while maintaining a pivotal and influential Role in the balance of Power & Trade throughout Oceania.

## Brief Conspectus
Robust, hearty, hale, good-humored fellow in possession of a healthy, contagious sense of *joie de vivre*. Fair and conscientious in his dealings with persons of all walks of life, he is held in the highest regard by native Hawaiian and foreigner alike, and is universally revered by his subjects as the "Merry Monarch." The watchword of his reign has always been *Hoouli Lahui* (Increase of the People).

## Historiette
- Born to the accompaniment of thunder and lightning at the foot of the Punchbowl Crater, Oahu, November 16, 1836
- Grandson of Aikanaka, son of Kapaakea and Keohokalole, brother to Liliuokalani and Likelike
- Began formal education in 1851 at High Chiefs' Children's School, Honolulu, Amos Starr Cooke & Juliette Montague, Schoolmasters
- Married Julia Kapiolani, 1863
- Elected King of All Hawaii by the Legislature, 1874
- Established reciprocity treaty with United States, 1876

## Tours & Travels
### American Tour, 1874–1875:
Sailed to San Francisco aboard *S.S. Benicia* in December and held audience with President U. S. Grant in Washington, D.C. in December. Returned to Honolulu February 1875 aboard *U.S.S. Pensacola*.

▶ *First reigning foreign monarch to ever set foot on U.S. soil.*

### World Tour, 1881:
Embarked January 20, 1881, accompanied by C. H. Judd (Chamberlain) & W. N. Armstrong (Minister of State), and the bibulous butler Baron von Oehlhoffen (Poet Laureate). Itinerary included:

Tokyo, Peking, Tientsin, Singapore, Calcutta, Aden, Cairo, Alexandria, Naples, Vienna, Berlin, London, Belfast, New York.

Audiences held with: • Emperor Mutsuhito of Japan • General Li Hung Chang of China •The Sultan of Johore (Siam) • Khedive Tewfik Pasha of Egypt • King Umberto & Queen Margherita of Italy • Pope Leo XIII • The Prince of Prussia • Queen Victoria • President Chester A. Arthur

*Illustration by Bart Doe*

# EMMETT KELLY

C/O PETE IODICE, NEW YORK OR
COLE BROS.-CLYDE BEATTY COMBINED CIRCUS
WINTER QUARTERS, ROCHESTER, INDIANA

## SITUATION SOUGHT

Seeking to contract for a lasting engagement as a *General Clown* with a better traveling variety show or well-received & established *Circus* (three rings preferred), or perhaps a truck or mud show, depending on the immediate situation, and if it has a decent cookhouse.

## NARRATIVE EXPOSITORY

Nearly 20 years in development, the persona of Weary Willie found form in 1933 with the Hagenbeck-Wallace Circus. Willie evolved from the European idea of the disreputable auguste and the tramp clown of vaudeville to the hobo juggler characterization (so well personified by the portraiture of W. C. Fields) and continued the metamorphosis with the development of the chalk-talk, the lightning cartoon, the Toby, the Bumpkin, and white-face (zinc oxide and lard).

## SYLLABUS OF CIRCUS HISTORY

⁂ First bitten by the bug when the Mighty Haag Show (Harry James, Cornetist), M. L. Clark and Sons Combined Shows, and the Brown & White Lyceum played Houston, Yukon, and Cabool, Missouri

⁂ *Single Trapeze Aerialist/Clown*, Howe's Great London Circus, 1922

⁂ Joined John Robinson's Circus and introduced *"The Aerial Kellys"* with wife Eva, 1923–1928

⁂ *Aerialist*, Sells-Floto Circus, 1929–1931

⁂ *General Clown*, Hagenbeck-Wallace Circus, 1931–1933

⁂ *Clown*, Cole Bros.–Clyde Beatty Combined Circus, 1934–1935

⁂ Engaged by Bertram Mills London Olympia Circus, London, England, for Christmas season this year

Other professional situations have included the Mighty Haag Show, Rogers & Harris, Frisco Exposition Shows of Kansas City, the St. Louis Police Circus, Irene Lackman's Dog & Pony Show, and cartoon acts on the nightclub circuit

## SPECIALIZATIONS

⁂ *"Shorty" Flemm's Spotlight Routine*

⁂ *Melting Ice w/Otto Griebling*

⁂ *The Peanut & Sledgehammer*

⁂ *WPA Shovel Routine w/Otto Griebling*

⁂ *Home Brew Outfit*

⁂ *Blueprint & Board*

*Testimonials & Character References are available from Bernard Mills, Clyde Beatty, Tom Mix, John Ringling, "Cheerful" Gardner, Terrell Jacobs, or any members of the Shifters Club*

# Queen Lydia Liliuokalani

*(Lydia Kamakaeha Paki)*
*Iolani Palace*
*364 South King Street*
*Honolulu, Kingdom of Hawaii*

## Royal Decree

To enlist popular support among the fair and just American people concerning President Grover Cleveland's righteous decision to oppose annexation of the Kingdom of Hawaii by the United States, and to recognize and sanction the present constitutional monarchy of the Kingdom and its reigning sovereign.

## Royal Delineation

Revered, respected, and honored by her subjects and ardently supported by the Royalist faction in her endeavor to create a new Hawaiian Constitution, as well as furthering the cause of "Hawaii for Hawaiians," Her Majesty is steadfast in her determination to maintain the monarchy as being in the best interest of her subjects. In possession of a refined regal bearing and singular grace of manner, she is held in the highest esteem by both the Hawaiian people and members of the foreign community.

## A Brief Synopsis of the Reign, & Certain Accomplishments Pertaining Thereto

❖ Proclaimed Queen of Hawaii January 29, 1891, upon the death of King Kalakaua, her brother, having been designated heir apparent in 1887
❖ Served as Regent during the King's world tour, 1881
❖ Legislated bills regarding Chinese immigration, opium licensing, and the proposed state lottery during 1892 session
❖ Drafted and submitted new state constitution, January 1893
❖ Princess Victoria Kaiulani, Kalaninuiahilapalapa Kawekiu i Lunalilo proclaimed heir apparent March 9, 1891

## Personal Historiette

❖ Born September 2, 1838, daughter of High Chief Kapaakea and the Chiefess Keohokalole; great-grandfather Keawe-a-Heulu was first cousin of the father of Kamehameha I; adopted at birth by Abner Paki, councillor of Kamehameha III, and his wife, Konia, grand-daughter of Kamehameha I
❖ Educated at High Chiefs' Children's School (renamed Royal School in 1846), 1842–1848, Amos S. Cooke, Master, and at Rev. Mr. Edward G. Beckwith's day school; studied English language & grammar, Christian fundamentals, Greek history, music, arithmetic, composition
❖ Travels include American tour, 1878, and second American visit (audience with President Cleveland) and journey to England for Grand Jubilee of Queen Victoria, 1887

*"I, Liliuokalani, by the Grace of God and under the Constitution of the Kingdom, do hereby solemnly protest against any and all acts done against myself and the constitutional Government of the Hawaiian Kingdom by certain persons claiming to have established a provisional government of and for this Kingdom."*

# JACK LONDON

*962 East 16th Street*
*Oakland, California*

## Statement of Occupational Intent & Nature of Situation Sought

A remunerative position that will effectively utilize natural literary and language talents and abilities, ideally in a field related to correspondence or journalism. Employment offers entailing manual labor will not be considered.

## Concise Background Narrative

A youth spent in wandering, restless adventure coalesced with inborn literary brilliance to produce the rare and exceptional talents in the possession of this remarkable young man. Any number of literary luminaries fortunate enough to have been exposed to these talents will readily attest, irrefragably, to the high quality and sincerity of the gifts displayed by this young scribe standing, as he is, on the threshold of a great career.

## Schooling & Formal Instruction

- University of California, Berkeley, 1896
- University Academy, Alameda, 1896
- Oakland High School, Oakland, 1895
- Cole Grammar School, West Oakland, 1887 (Class Historian)
- Franklin School, Oakland, 1886
- Garfield School, Oakland, 1885
- Livermore School, Livermore, 1883
- West End School, Alameda, 1882

## Employment History

- **Gold Prospector** in the Klondike, 1897–1898
- **Laundryman**, Belmont Academy Laundry, 1897
- **Work Beast**, Oakland, San Leandro, and Hayward Electric Railway, 1894
- **Sailor Before the Mast**, *Sophia Sutherland*, 1893
- **Deputy** to Charley LeGrant, California Fish Patrol, Benicia, 1892
- **Owner/Operator**, *Razzle Dazzle*, (oyster-sloop), 1891
- **Labor Swink**, Hickmott's Cannery, Oakland, 1889

## Literary Accomplishments to Date

Accepted for publication: *A Thousand Deaths*, **Black Cat** magazine, Boston, Mass., H.D. Umbstatter, Editor (to be published May 1899)

*Two Gold Bricks*, **Owl Magazine**, September 1897

Articles published in **The Aegis**, student literary magazine, Oakland High School:

- *Optimism, Pessimism, and Patriotism*
- *One More Unfortunate*
- *Frisco Kid*
- *Sakaicho Hona Asi and Hakadaki*
- *Who Believes in Ghosts?*
- *Bonin Islands*
- *And Frisco Kid Came Back*

First prize in contest sponsored by the **San Francisco Morning Call**: *Story of a Typhoon Off the Coast of Japan*, November 1893

## Memberships & Affiliations

- Henry Clay Debating Society • American Section, Socialist Labor Party

## Character References

- Johnny Heinold, owner, Heinold's First & Last Chance Saloon, Webster Street, Oakland
- Ina Donna Coolbrith, Librarian, Oakland Public Library • Mrs. Jenny Prentiss, Oakland

HISTORIC RESUMES OF FAMOUS AMERICANS

# Senator Huey Long

## State Capitol Building
## Riverside Mall and Boyd Avenue
## New Orleans, Louisiana

## "Every Man a King, but No One Wears a Crown"

### Political Plan & Prospectus

To continue to nurture, advocate, and promote the ever-growing **Share Our Wealth** movement by bringing it to every city, village, farm, factory, and humble hearthside in the land and to actively embark on a **Third Party Presidential Campaign** in anticipation of a landslide popular victory in 1936.

### Sum & Substance

Energetic, vigorous, potent, and charismatic political dynamo packed with a formidable charge of social dynamite and possessed of a fiery invective regarding his proposed radically corrective readjustment of the means of distribution of wealth in the United States; outspoken and forthright, he has made enormous inroads concerning the social betterment, progress, and well-being of the people in the State of Louisiana, a representative listing of which includes:

- *Roads & Bridges:* As Governor and Senator, more than doubled the improved road mileage in Louisiana from 1928 to the present. Major highway bridges totaled 3 in 1928; this year there are more than 40.
- *Schools:* Significantly increased school allotments, instituted free schoolbook program, reduced the state's illiteracy rate by half, and improved Louisiana State University's Intercollegiate Association of State Universities classification from third rate to A-Number 1.
- *Hospitals:* Doubled patient care facilities in certain hospitals and reduced death rate by 50%.

### Political Chronology

☆ *Graduate,* Tulane University Law School, New Orleans, 1915
☆ *State Railroad Commissioner* (Northern District), 1918–1920
☆ *Chairman,* Public Service Commission, 1921–1926
☆ *Governor,* State of Louisiana, 1928–1932
☆ *United States Senator,* 1932–Present

### Share Our Wealth Society Facts & Figures

• Share-the-Wealth proposal first introduced in the Senate, March 1932 • 27,000 Share Our Wealth Clubs nationwide • 1935 Membership: 4,684,000 • Mailing List: 7,500,000

• Guaranteed minimum annual income! • Every family furnished a homestead allowance! • No excessive personal fortunes! • Guaranteed old-age pensions! • Equal education for all!

*No Tinpot Napoleon, Stump-Jumping Demagogue, or Proto-Fascist Dictator, Huey Long is the Great Commoner & Leader of the Masses, the People's Choice for President in 1936!*

# Juliette Gordon Low

Girl Scouts National Headquarters
Munsey Building, Washington, D.C.
~or~
142 Bull Street
Savannah, Georgia

### Ultimate Aim & Purpose
To promote, encourage, cultivate, and otherwise develop the Girl Guiding movement
in the United States and to create a nationwide brigade that will embody similar
principles to those currently being practiced by the Girl Guide and Boy Scout
organizations in Great Britain.

### Concise Personal Conspectus
Vigorous, energetic, and resolute woman with pronounced qualities of eternal
youthfulness and creative eccentricity; a rare original thinker possessing a single-minded,
iron-willed determination to create an organization that will provide a means of healthy
and positive development and education related to the nurturing of practical & useful
skills, crafts, and general know-how for American girls from all stations of life.

### Encapsulated Historiette
❀ West Hull Street School, Savannah, 1867–1868
❀ Stuart Hall Academy, Staunton, Virginia, 1874–1875
❀ Graduate, Edge Hill Academy, Charlottesville, Virginia, 1877
❀ Member, "Theta Taus"
❀ Mesdemoiselles Charbonnier's School, New York City, 1877
❀ Additional studies, Dodsworth Dancing Academy
❀ Married William Mackay Low, December 1886; established residence at
   Wellesbourne House, Warwickshire, England
❀ Spanish-American War Relief Volunteer/Nurse, Florida, 1898
❀ Founded Girl Guides troops in Glen Lyon, Scotland, & London, England, 1911
❀ Organized first American Girl Guides troop, Savannah, March 1912
   (renamed Girl Scouts)

### A Brief Listing of Certain Appreciations, Applications,
### and Considerations of the Organization
✦ Agriculture ✦ Handicrafts ✦ Practical Outdoor Skills ✦ Cooking & Home Sciences
✦ First Aid ✦ Art Appreciation ✦ Sewing ✦ Nutrition & Hygiene ✦ Athletics
✦ Appreciation of the Natural World ✦ Practical Mechanical Skills Development
✦ Music and Dance ✦ Leadership Development ✦ Career Planning ✦ International Studies
Publication in Progress: *How Girls Can Help Their Country*

### Representative Roster of Persons Offering
### Support and Encouragement
✦ General Sir Robert Baden-Powell ✦ Rudyard Kipling ✦ Mrs. Woodrow Wilson
✦ Jane Addams ✦ His Highness The Prince of Wales

"IT IS BETTER TO BE A REAL GIRL SUCH AS NO BOY CAN POSSIBLY BE."

# Aimee Semple McPherson

**c/o International Church of the Foursquare Gospel**
Angelus Temple, Echo Park, Los Angeles, California

## Divine Mission

To spread the Joyous **Word** of **God** to people of every kindred, tribe, and tongue, to proclaim **Jesus Christ** the same Yesterday, Today, and Forever, and to bring the people of all nations to a personal knowledge of **Jesus the Saviour**, the **Great Physician**, the **Baptizer** with the **Holy Spirit**, and the **Soon Coming King**.

## Summarized Compilation of Characteristics

*"Sister" McPherson was called early in life to exalt Jesus Christ as the Way, the Truth, and the Life throughout the world. She never swerved from her dedication to reach suffering humanity with the love and compassion of her Lord. Packed churches, auditoriums, arenas, theaters, and the Madison Square Gardens as well as the Royal Albert Hall in England with crowds reaching as high as 80,000 all bore witness to those seeking salvation, healing, and deliverance through her ministry. As an outstanding pioneer and flaming evangelist, she crossed the United States eight times from 1918 through 1923, later encircling the globe a number of times and visiting the five continents in an effort to pray for those in need. Her sought-after message and ministry brought hope to millions. Her God-given talents in oratory and song administered fervent, militant mass evangelism and spectacular pageantry, drawing even the most recalcitrant of lost souls. With every breath she drew she welcomed every opportunity to lead people to Christ, pray for their healing and infilling of the Holy Spirit, and prepare for His coming.*

## Personal Histioriography

- Born October 9, 1890, Ingersoll, Ontario, Canada, only daughter of the Kennedys, active Salvation Army soldiers
- Exposed to theatre, novel reading, worldly entertainments, habits of fancy dress, and high school dances until "...I became practically an infidel"
- Reborn through the Holy Spirit by receiving Jesus Christ as personal Saviour at the age of 17
- Married evangelist Robert Semple, 1908
- Robert Semple called Home to the Lord, Hong Kong, China, 1910
- Returned to America with daughter Roberta to minister and continue carrying the torch; married Harold McPherson; son Rolf born

## Missionary Travels

- Throughout the United States
- Australia & New Zealand
- Canada
- Central & South America
- China, Japan, & the Philippines
- India & Africa
- Ireland & England
- Israel

## Creations, Accomplishments, and Publications

† Founded the Echo Park Evangelistic Association, Inc., 1921

† Established and built Angelus Temple, seating 5,300, in Los Angeles, California, 1923

† Founded KFSG, third oldest radio station in Los Angeles, 1924; established L.I.F.E. Bible College, 1925

† Composed 200 songs, seven (two-hour) sacred operas, & three children's Christmas plays

† Preached 21 times per week while ministering in the Angelus Temple; presented her famous "illustrated sermons"

† Organized the Angelus Temple Commissary Department, which fed and clothed 1,500,000 persons

† Founded the Angelus Temple Prayer Tower from which an average of 17,000 calls per month were received and prayed over by men & women in two-hour shifts, 24 hours per day

† Published *The Bridal Call* and *Foursquare Crusader* (periodicals) and *This Is That*, book of sermons, 1923, as well as five other books and many smaller works dealing with cardinal doctrines of faith

Herman Melville

# Herman Melville

**104 East 26th Street**
**New York City, New York**

### *Nature of Situation Sought*

A sound, steadfast, and permanent governmental post, preferably with the Customs–House in this city, which would serve to benefit from the active application of the wide and divergent worldly experiences of the Principal.

### *Epitomized Profile*

Proficient, successful, and renowned author of adventurous and imaginative fiction based on actuality of experience, which is written with vigor and originality in a distinctive allegorical fashion; an adequate education received as a young man and the performance of duty at numerous miscellaneous stations of responsible employment lends credence to suitability for a bureaucratic assignment.

### *Scholastic Pupilarities*

• New York Male High School, 1826–1830 • Albany Academy (History / Ciphering / Classical Biography / Jewish Antiquities —First Best in Class, Ciphering), 1830–1832 • Albany Classical School (Literature), 1835–1837 • Lansingburgh Academy (Surveying), 1838 • Member, Philo Logos Society

### *Compendious Historiography of Employments*

- **Bank Clerk/Farm Laborer/Factory Worker**, 1832–1837
- **Schoolmaster**, Sykes District School, Pittsfield, Massachusetts, 1837 and Greenbush & Schodack Academy, Greenbush, New York, 1839–1840
- **Seaman**, the *St. Lawrence*, New York–Liverpool, 1839
- **Common Seaman**, the South Seas whaler *Acushnet*, 1841–1842
- **Clerk**, Issac Montgomery, Merchant; Honolulu, Sandwich Islands, 1843
- **Ordinary Seaman**, United States Navy, 1843–1844
- **Professional Wordsmith**, 1845–Present
- **Gentleman Farmer**, Arrowhead Farm, Pittsfield, Mass., 1850–1863
- **Travelling Lecturer**, 1857–1860 (Topics: "The South Seas"; "Statuary in Rome"; "Travelling")

### *Published Literary Works*

• *Typee: A Peep at Polynesian Life During a Four Months Residence in a Valley of the Marquesas*, 1846 • *Omoo, a Narrative of Adventures in the South Seas*, 1847 • *Mardi, and a Voyage Thither*, 1848 • *Redburn*, 1848 • *White-Jacket, or the World in a Man-of-War*, 1850 • *Moby Dick, or the White Whale*, 1851 • *Pierre, or the Ambiguities*, 1852 • *Israel Potter, His Fifty Years of Exile*, 1855 • *The Piazza Tales*, 1856 • *The Confidence Man*, 1857 • *Battle-Pieces, and Aspects of the War*, 1866

TESTIMONIES PERTAINING TO CHARACTER, SOBER HABITS, AND DESIRABLE DEGREE OF PROFESSIONALISM AVAILABLE FROM CHIEF JUSTICE LEMUEL SHAW OF BOSTON; EVERT DUYCKINCK, EDITOR, NEW YORK CITY; OLIVER WENDELL HOLMES, BOSTON

# Billy Mitchell

BOXWOOD FARM,
MIDDLEBURG, VIRGINIA

## Statement of Intent

To educate and enlighten the American people concerning the crucial issues of modern defense as regards the backward and archaic state of military aviation, the mossback mentalities, and the pronounced lack of modernization, advanced aircraft, and progressive theory & policies, and to seek private funding for establishment of the University of Aviation, which will instruct modern Military Aviation Theory & Practice at an educational level equal to West Point and Annapolis.

## Studied Foresight and Observation

The United States is currently in a position of present and future peril from foreign enemies whose evil intentions are yet to be fully perceived. Industrialization & modernization ushered in a new era of warfare during the European Conflict, and it is of utmost importance that American military policymakers look to the future, a future that will most assuredly include combat aircraft playing significant strategic roles.

## Prognostication

That the United States and its allies will, within the decade, be gravely threatened by rising European military powers equipped with formidable airborne striking capabilities as well as by the Empire of Japan which, even now, is producing great ships designed to deliver crushing airborne attack forces from enormous distances. Seventeen Japanese factories have been reported working around the clock since 1923 producing military aircraft. There is a distinct possibility that American military bases in the Territory of Hawaii and in the Philippine Islands will be at great risk.

## Military Background

- Enlisted, Company M, 1st Wisconsin Infantry Regiment, Wisconsin National Guard, April 1898
- Assigned to Signal Corps as 2nd Lieutenant, August 1898. Served in Cuba, the Philippines, and Territory of Alaska; promoted to Captain, 1903
- Attended Army Staff College (Publication: *Our Faulty Military Policy*)
- Youngest member of the General Staff, 1912; assigned to Aviation Section of the Signal Corps, 1915
- Promoted to Brigadier General, September 1918, while serving as Air Commander in France; successfully conducted mass bombing raid behind German lines with 1,481 attack aircraft
- Successfully demonstrated air power potential by sinking captured battleships during controlled tests, 1921 & 1923
- Established new air speed record of 224.38 mph, October 1922
- Court-martialed for violations of the 98th Article of War, December 1925. Witnesses for the defense included Eddie Rickenbacker, Carl Spaatz, Major H. H. Arnold, and Congressman Fiorello LaGuardia of New York
- Resigned army commission, January 28, 1926

# Tom Mix

| | | |
|---|---|---|
| 1018 Summit Drive | | Sells-Floto Circus |
| Beverly Hills | -or- | Winter Quarters |
| California | | Peru, Indiana |

---

### Manifesto of Histrionic Diversification or,
### The Plan to Rove on the Road with a Traveling Show

Now that the talkies seem here to stay, it is the intent of the cowboy star to satisfy a mighty powerful hankerin' to leave the bright lights of Hollywood behind, load up the horse, organize some gear, and get back out on the sawdust trail under a big top.

### Capitulation of Circus & Other Successes, Past & Present

☆ Zack Mulhall's Wild West Show, St. Louis Exposition, 1904

☆ Ring Stock Foreman/Cowboy, Miller Brothers' 101 Real Wild West Ranch, Ponca City, Oklahoma, 1906–1909

☆ National Rodeo Riding Championships: Prescott, Arizona, 1909; Canon City, Colorado, 1911

☆ Tom Mix Wild West Show, Western Washington Fair, Seattle, Washington • Kit Carson Buffalo Ranch • Widerman Wild West Show • Will A. Dickey's Circle D Wild West Show and Indian Congress

☆ Arena Director, Guy Weadick/Fred T. Cummins Wild West Show, Calgary, Alberta, Canada, 1912–1913

☆ European Wild West Tour, 1925: Belgium, England (audience with the Lord Mayor of London), France, Germany, Holland

☆ Sells-Floto Circus (American Circus Corporation), 1929–1932

☆ Tom Mix Round-Up (w/Tony the Wonder Horse, some Liberty Ponies, a rope-spinning act, and the Ward Sisters), 1933

### Brief Epitome of Moving Picture Accomplishments That Have Led to the
### Establishment of an International Reputation of Esteem & Renown

★ Signed with the Selig Polyscope Company, 1910. Early flickers included "Ranch Life in the Great Southwest," with Old Blue (retired 1914), and "The Heart of Texas Ryan," with Tony the Wonder Horse.

★ Foreign films include the Danish productions of "Den Glade Tom" ("The Conversion of Smiling Tom") and "Hest Contra Bil" ("Taking A Chance").

★ Contracted to Fox Films, 1918; starred in over 70 oaters through 1927; made a series of silents for Film Booking Office, 1928–1929; starred in nine films produced by Universal, 1932–1933

### Additional Early Information, or
### Life Before Show Business

• United States Artillery, Batteries M & O, 1898–1902 (Final rank: 1st Sergeant)
• Bartender, Blue Belle Saloon, Guthrie, Oklahoma, 1904 • Deputy Sheriff/Night Marshal, Dewey, Oklahoma, 1905 • Honorary Texas Ranger
• Drum Major, Oklahoma Cavalry Band

John Muir

# John Muir

c/o Postmaster, Alhambra Valley
Martinez, California

## Purpose and Intent

To enlist Public Support in the cause of the Preservation & Protection of the Hetch Hetchy Valley, "The Tuolumne Yosemite," or, as it is sometimes known, "Smith's Valley," which is being threatened by a proposed dam on the Tuolumne River. "Tidings from far & near show that almost every good man and woman is with us in this fight."

## Personal Profile

❦ True and Accomplished Naturalist, Conservationist, and Mountaineer ❦
❦ Proficient & Productive Journalist, Correspondent, and Author of
Numerous Works meant to Promote the Preservation of Natural Environments
for the Public Good ❦
❦ Robust Outdoorsman & Lover of the Sublime Wilderness ❦
❦ Dedicated to Spreading the Big Bound Pages of Mountain Gospel
Written with the same Pen of Ice which the Lord long ago Passed
over every Page of the Great Sierra Nevada ❦

## Biographical Epitome

❖ Emigrated from Scotland, 1849; attended University of Wisconsin 1860–1863
❖ Invented & produced numerous useful mechanical devices including: ◆ An Early Rising Machine ◆ Wooden Mechanical Clocks ◆ Thermometers ◆ Hygrometers ◆ Pyrometers ◆ Barometers ◆ An Automatic Fire Lighter ◆ Mechanical Desk
❖ *Employments:* Meaford Broom Handle Co., Meaford, Ontario, 1863–1865
Osgood, Smith, & Company Manufactory, Indianapolis, 1866
❖ Thousand Mile Walk to the Gulf of Mexico, 1867; sailed to San Francisco, 1868
❖ Established theory of glacial origin of the Yosemite Valley; initially disputed and ridiculed by the geological academic community, the theories were proven correct.
❖ *Travels:* Alaska ◆ Siberia ◆ Manchuria ◆ Himalayas ◆ Africa ◆ China ◆ New Zealand ◆ Australia ◆ South Seas ◆ Japan ◆ South America
❖ First President of the Sierra Club (Founded 1892)
❖ Honorary degrees received from University of California, Harvard, Yale, and the University of Wisconsin

## Publications

*The Yosemite*, 1912 ◆ *Our National Parks*, 1901 ◆ *The Mountains of California*, 1894
◆ *The Story of My Boyhood and My Youth* ◆ *My First Summer in the Sierra*
◆ Numerous articles published in *Century Magazine, Scribner's Monthly, Harper's Weekly, Atlantic Monthly, Overland Monthly*, & *New York Daily Tribune*

## Commendations and Endorsements

◆ Theodore Roosevelt ◆ William Howard Taft
◆ Mrs. Ezra Slocum Carr of Wisconsin ◆ Robert U. Johnson, Editor

# Carry Amelia Moore Nation
### Rural Route 2, Guthrie, Oklahoma Territory

## Statement of Intent

To secure Public Support and Sponsorship of an Amendment to the United States Constitution that would prohibit Production, Importation, and Consumption of any and all Ardent Spirits and Potations, including beer, wine, whiskey, shine, and forty-rod, into, about, and of the American Republic and all its Territories.

## Vignette of Sum and Substance

Truculent and garrulous woman of commanding stature and presence possessed of an active and vigorous invective and a burning, furious passion to zealously crusade in the faithful service of the divinely ordained mission which is her life. All strength and energies focused into an unyielding enmity to all forms of intoxicating liquors and the corrupt purveyors thereof. Well versed and experienced in the direct, rather unorthodox methods of presenting her convictions to the general public.

## Brief Biographical Discourse

Born November 25, 1846, in Garrard County, Kentucky, the issue of the union of George Moore, prosperous planter, and Mary Campbell Moore, an unfortunate woman suffering grandiose delusions of Royal origin. Family fortunes were obliterated by the onset of the War Between the States, necessitating numerous relocations throughout Kentucky, Missouri, and Texas.

Educated by tutors, various public & private institutions, and the State Normal School, Warrensburg, Missouri; received much inspiration through the animistic beliefs and practices of Negro slaves.
- Married Charles Gloyd, 1867 (Widowed by Demon Rum within the year)
- Teacher, State Normal School, Holden, Missouri, 1868–1872
- Married David Nation, Editor, *The Warrensburg Journal*, 1877
- Hotel Manager, Columbia and Richmond, Texas, 1879–1889
- Established residence in Medicine Lodge, Kansas, 1889

## Hatchetations, Disruptions, & Joint Smashing Escapades

☀ Disarranged Mart Strong's place, Medicine Lodge, Kansas, 1899 ☀ First Joint Smashing: Kiowa, Kansas, May 1900 ☀ Wrecked the Hotel Carey Ballroom, Wichita, December 1900 ☀ Demolished the Senate Saloon, Topeka, 1901 ☀ Invaded & disrupted Governor's Chambers, Topeka, 1902 ☀ Further joint smashings at Enterprise, Danville, Winfield, and Leavenworth, Kansas, as well as New York City, Washington, D.C., Rochester, N.Y., and San Francisco; arrested more than 30 times.

## Related Accomplishments

- Published autobiography, *The Use and Need of the Life of Carry A. Nation*, 1904, as well as the periodicals *The Smasher's Mail*, *The Hatchet*, and *The Home Defender*
- Conducted East Coast lecture tour under the sponsorship of the Furlong Lyceum Bureau of Rochester, 1901
- Built the Home for the Wives and Mothers of Drunkards, Kansas City
- Appeared onstage in the dramatization of *Hatchetation (Ten Nights in a Bar-Room)*, Elizabeth, New Jersey

# ANNIE OAKLEY
### 300 Grant Avenue, Nutley, New Jersey

## Nature of Situation Sought

A suitable theatrical endeavor that will fully exploit the world-renowned feats, achievements, and cunning histrionics expertly displayed by this seasoned performer.

## Epitome

"The Peerless Lady Wing-Shot," or, as rendered in the Sioux tongue, "Wan-Tan-Yeya-Ci-Sci-La" (Little Sureshot), is revered around the globe for her uncanny, nearly magical skill with rifle and pistol. Clean-living and frugal, she offers an exemplary role model for the young as well as a refreshing and invigorating "persona" to children of all ages.

## Biographical Summation

Born in Woodland, Darke County, Ohio, August 13, 1860
Delegated to Darke County Orphanage, 1869
Adopted 1870, ran away 1872
Reunited with mother, North Star Township, 1872
Earned a living as game provider and paid off farm mortgage, 1874
Married Frank Butler, showman/manager, 1876

## Historiette of Public Life

• Show-business career launched with an upset victory over future husband in a shooting match at the *Schuetzenbuckle*, or Shooter's Hill, Cincinnati, 1875

• Toured as "Butler & Oakley," 1876–1881

• Joined Sells Brothers' Circus, "The Biggest of All Shows," and performed at the World's Industrial & Cotton Centennial Exposition (The Biggest Exhibit, The Biggest Building, The Biggest Industrial Event in the World's History), New Orleans, 1884–1885

• Began 17-year association with Buffalo Bill Cody and the Rocky Mountain and Prairie Exhibition (later Wild West Show & Congress of Rough Riders), New Orleans, April 1885

## Seventeen Years with the Wild West Show

1885–1886:  Eastern U.S. and Canadian Tour

1887–1888:  European Tour including Earl'scourt Exhibition Grounds, London, and audience with Queen Victoria. Command performance for the German Emperor, Charlottenburg, Fall 1887

1889–1890:  Second European Tour included Exposition Universel, Paris, 1889. Played Rome, Florence, Milan, Verona, Venice, Switzerland, Germany, Austria

1891–1892:  Tour of Scotland & England

1892–1893:  World's Columbian Exposition, Chicago

1894:  U.S. Tour

## Additional Engagements

• Pawnee Bill's Frontier Exhibition, 1888 • Tony Pastor's Opera House, New York, 1887–1888 & 1892 • Nutley Charity Circus (Red Cross Relief), 1894 • Rejoined the Wild West Show, 1889

FROM THE AUTOGRAPH BOOK: "To the loveliest and truest little woman, both in heart and aim in all the world. Sworn to by and before myself."
—*W. F. (Buffalo Bill) Cody*, Strasbourg, 1890

# J. Robert Oppenheimer

c/o The Athenaeum, California Institute of Technology
551 South Hill Avenue, Pasadena, California

## STATEMENT OF PURPOSE

To enlist the support of the physical sciences community regarding the application and furtherance of the recent significant scientific advances concerning atomic fission and the ultimate enormous impact these discoveries could conceivably have on the development of military weapons. Urgent action is deemed appropriate at this time as war in Europe appears imminent.

## CURSORY THEORETICAL DELINEATION FOR THE LAYMAN

Since the atom was split in 1931, enormous inroads have been made concerning the understanding of the reactive properties of the atoms of certain elements (specifically uranium) when the nucleus is bombarded with neutrons. A resultant activity, called a "chain reaction," has now been confirmed by the French, but is not at this time fully understood. There is theory that this chain reaction may not be confined solely to the target element and could progress instantaneously into the atoms of other elements, including nitrogen (composing 80% of the Earth's atmosphere). Simply put, it is not outside the realm of possibility that, upon initiation of the chain reaction, all physical matter could cease to exist within a millisecond. Therefore, it would seem imperative that all atomic weapons research be suspended until war, or the threat of war, has passed.

## CURRICULUM VITAE

✦ Graduate, Ethical Culture School, Central Park West, New York City

✦ A.B. (Summa Cum Laude), Chemistry, Harvard College, June 1925

✦ Christ's College, University of Cambridge, September 1925–August 1926
  • Physics research at Cavendish Laboratory under Prof. J. J. Thomson
  • Quantum theory papers published, *Journal of the Cambridge Philosophical Society*, 1926

✦ Ph.D., Physics, University of Göttingen, March 1927

✦ National Research Council Fellow:
  • Harvard University, September–December 1927
  • California Institute of Technology, January–July 1928
  • Universities of Leiden & Utrecht, September–December 1928
  • Eidgenossiche Technische Hochschule, Zurich, January–June 1929

✦ Assistant Professor of Physics, California Institute of Technology, Pasadena, and University of California, Berkeley (concurrent appointments August 1929)
  • Promoted to Associate Professor, U.C. & C.I.T., October 1931
  • Full Professorships, U.C. & C.I.T., August 1936

## COLLEAGUES

❋ Carl Anderson ❋ Hans Bethe ❋ Niels Bohr ❋ Max Born ❋ Enrico Fermi ❋ Werner Heisenberg ❋ Ernest O. Lawrence ❋ Robert Serber ❋ Edward Teller ❋ John van Vleck

# Satchel Paige

c/o J. L. (Ralph) Wilkinson, Owner
Kansas City Monarchs
420 East 9th Street
Kansas City, Missouri

## Plan of Action

Now that the arm seems to have fixed itself, the applicant wishes to secure a starting pitching position with an "A" or "1st" list Negro Leagues team in one of the larger venues in the Midwest or East.

## Summation of Athletic Prowess

Maybe the fastest pitcher in the nation, maybe even the fastest pitcher in the history of the game, he also possesses control that will allow him to put seven out of ten fastballs in a strike zone the size of a gum wrapper. Struck out 22 Babe Ruth All-Star major leaguers in a barnstorm game in Los Angeles, 1930.

*"Satchel and me would be worth a quarter million to any major league club…between us we'd win sixty games."*—Dizzy Dean

*"Satchel Paige is the best pitcher I have ever faced."*—Joe DiMaggio

## Representative List of Famous Deliveries

• Bee Ball • Pea Ball • Eephus Pitch •
• Hesitation Pitch • Bat Dodger • Long Tom •
• Jump Ball • Wobbly Ball • Trouble Ball •
• Drooper • Two–Hump Blooper •
*(But never a shine ball, emery ball, needle ball, or spitter)*

## Compendium of Certifiable Authenticities of Prowess & Proficiency on the Mound

- W. H. Council School, Mobile, Alabama…struck out 16 batters first game
- Industrial School for Negro Children, Mt. Meigs, Alabama…pitcher
- Mobile Tigers, 1923–1925…30-game winner, 1924
- Chattanooga Black Lookouts, 1926
- Birmingham Black Barons, 1927…18 strikeouts, first game
- Nashville Elite Giants, 1928–1930…generally 12–20 strikeouts per game
- Pittsburgh Crawfords, 1931–1934…streak: 21 straight wins, 64 scoreless innings
- All-White Independent League, Bismarck, North Dakota, 1935…pitched 29 games in one month
- Satchel Paige All-Stars, Winter 1935

AND NUMEROUS PITCHING ENGAGEMENTS FOR A WIDE VARIETY OF LATIN AMERICAN TEAMS IN VENEZUELA, MEXICO, CUBA, AND PUERTO RICO AS WELL AS RAFAEL TRUJILLO'S ALL-STARS IN THE DOMINICAN REPUBLIC

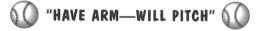 "HAVE ARM—WILL PITCH"

# DOROTHY PARKER

57 West 57th Street
New York, New York

**Intent**

Now that wages are coming down, the applicant wishes to alert Mr. Harold Ross, c/o Algonquin Hotel, West 44th Street, this city, of her intention to secure a suitable position, station, or post with his proposed new magazine, which will assuredly provide Croesus-like remuneration and stellar fame while best utilizing her clever, erudite, and adroit talents, but that, for the sake of appearances, should not bear even the slightest resemblance to gainful employment.

**Profile**

Sophisticated, cosmopolitan, and urbane, but by no means high brow; irreverent and a bit flippant, but shouldn't be construed as radical; merry and gay, but regularly provides an ever-so-quick glimpse at a dark side; possesses pronounced indications of what could be interpreted as a quick and ready wit.

**Previous Situations**

**Condé Nast Publications**, New York, New York
**1915–January 1920**

- Editorial Cub/Caption Writer, **Vogue**, Edna Woodman Chase, Editor,
Graybar Building, 43rd Street New York
Published several hate songs, including "**Any Porch**"

- Caption Writer/Theatre Critic, **Vanity Fair**, Frank Crowninshield,
Editor, 19 West 44th Street, New York
Wrote fillers, contents pages, and slugs; eventually assigned to theatre criticism (nom de plume Helène Rousseau) upon the departure of Alexander Woolcott. Panned certain productions of Florenz Ziegfeld, David Belasco, & Charles Dillingham, and as a result parted company with the magazine.

- Partner, Utica Drop Forge and Tool Company, Parkbench, New York, Benchley & Parker, Presidents
Weekly poetry published in **Life**, Edward S. Martin, Editor

**Freelance**

- **Ainslee's** • **Everybody's** • **Ladies' Home Journal** • **Saturday Evening Post**
(Short Turns and Encores) • **The Conning Tower** (New York Tribune)

**Education**

Miss Dana's School for Young Ladies, South Street, Morristown,
New Jersey, 1906–1910
Blessed Sacrament Academy (Sisters of Charity), West 79th Street, New York

**Memberships**

Thanatopsis Literary and Inside Straight Club
Vicious Circle, Algonquin Hotel, New York

# Quanah Parker
## c/o Office of Indian Affairs
## Fort Sill, Oklahoma

---

## Circumstance Sought
A situation that would suitably exploit natural gift of business acumen and discernment as well as uniquely individual hereditarial birthright.

## Compendium of Personal History
Accomplished businessman and negotiator as well as living link to the days of the free and wild American West; true personification of a viable embodiment of two distinct and diverse worlds whose natural leadership abilities are evidenced by lengthy successful command of Comanche warriors engaged in effective guerrilla operations as well as by eminently profitable business dealings concerning leasing of Indian lands to the Cattle Kings. Much honored and respected patriarch held in highest esteem by Indian and White alike.

## Personal Histioriography
- Born at Cedar Lake, Texas, May 1845
- Father: Peta Nocona, Chief of the Quahadi Band of the Comanche Tribe
- Mother: Cynthia Ann Parker, taken captive by the Comanche in May 1836 at the age of nine, renamed Preloch, and raised by the tribe to adulthood

## Combat and Battle Experience as War Chief of the Quahadi Band, 1867–1875
- Led an alliance of Comanche, Kiowa, Apache, and Cheyenne warriors in defiance of the Medicine Lodge Treaty of 1867
- Planned and executed numerous raids on settlements and frontier towns throughout the Texas Panhandle and the Indian Nations
- Commanded united Indian force at the Battle of Adobe Walls, 1874
- Honorably surrendered to General Ranald Mackenzie, 1875

## Business and Related Accomplishments as Pertaining to Adaptability to White Ways and Culture
- Rancher/Farmer, Indian Territory, 1876–Present
- Business Manager, Comanche/Kiowa/Apache Tribes, 1876–Present
- Presiding Judge, Court of Indian Affairs, 1886–1898

## Further Merits and Successes
• Leased surplus Indian lands to stock raisers and cattle companies, thus realizing income in excess of $100,000 yearly in the name of the Associated Tribes • Fluent in the Spanish and English languages, as well as traditional Indian dialects • Established numerous Indian educational institutions • Participated in President Theodore Roosevelt's inauguration parade, Washington, D.C., 1905

Copyright 1904
C.T. Tatman.

# Edgar Allan Poe

**c/o Mr. John Allan**
**Richmond, Virginia**

---

## Situation Desired

A position related to **Editing** or **Publishing** that would prove to be of mutual benefit both to the Gentleman and an employer by efficaciously applying rather unique creative abilities.

## Professional Delineation

Darkly prophetic visionary driven by mystical unseen forces to produce poetical and prose works that time will prove to be beyond the ken of mere mortals. Complex, somewhat confused personality given to fits of unexplained outburst accompanied by a blaze of creative output, which behavior remains baffling to phrenologists. Petulant, proud, solitary, labyrinthine dreamer driven to achieve immortality by the creation of timeless, melodic works, "like sweet bells jangled, out of tune and harsh."

## Education

*Primary Schools:*
- Irvine, Scotland, 1815
- Sloane Street, London, 1815–1816
- Manor House School, Stoke Newington, England, 1817–1820

*Preparatory School:*
- Richmond, Virginia, 1820–25

*College:*
- University of Virginia, February–December 1826
  –Studied Greek, Latin, French, Spanish, Italian
- United States Military Academy, West Point, 1830–1831

## Military Service

United States Army–Honorably Discharged, 1829
- Final Rank: Sergeant Major

## Publications

*Tamerlane and Other Poems*, 1827
*Al Aaraaf, Tamerlane, and Minor Poems*, 1829
*Poems,* 1831 (including "Israfel" and "The Doomed City")
*Metzengerstein,* 1832
–Received $50 prize for *MS. Found in a Bottle*, 1833

# The Pony Express

Advertisement of Intended Ownership Transference and
Prospectus of Established Enterprise, &c.; or,
Notice of Intent to Sell

## Name & Nature of the Business

The Central Overland Pony Express Company, exclusively engaged in the delivery of U.S. mail, by horseback, over an established route between St. Joseph, Missouri, and Sacramento, California.

## Brief Operational Summation

Swift and efficient delivery of First Class mail by dedicated and professional riders by way of unprecedented overland route. Operation supported by numerous established swing, relay, and home stations maintained at strategic locations. To date over 30,000 pieces of mail have been safely and timely delivered while suffering the loss of only one sack.

## Figures, Statistics, & Inventories

► $700,000 invested since April 1860
► Postage rates: $5.00 per ½ ounce at inception of service; reduced to $1.00, July 1861
► Average delivery time to Sacramento: 10 days (1,830 miles)
► 190 recently built relay stations; 500 prime horses, saddles, tack, leather cantinas, mochilas, etc.
► Pony Express employs only devoted, courageous, sober, and hard-working riders and support personnel
► U.S. Government public service subsidy currently being negotiated

*"No swifter, surer, more fearless messenger has ever sailed
the solid tide of the boundless Western prairie."* —Horace Greeley

## Proposed Terms & Negotiable Elements of Transference

The principals are willing to discuss and negotiate any and all reasonable offers and proposals from interested & qualified parties but must stress that all proceedings concerning sale and/or trade be completed before the end of the season, as inclement weather could delay required transfer or shipping of associated properties. Trades concerning related (or unrelated) business(es) will be carefully considered. Agents' inquiries & foreign queries accepted.

## Affiliates

● Russell, Majors & Waddell, Freighters, Leavenworth, Kansas Territory
● Leavenworth & Pike's Peak Express Company, St. Joseph, Missouri
● Central Overland, California & Pike's Peak Express

INTERESTED PARTIES CONTACT MESSRS. WM. H. RUSSELL, ALEXANDER MAJORS, OR
WM. B. WADDELL, ST. JOSEPH OR LEAVENWORTH

# Paul LeRoy Robeson

c/o Provincetown Players
133 MacDougal Street, Greenwich Village
New York, New York

## Situation Desired

A creative endeavor that would make full and effective use of the wide range of unique and singular talents in the possession of this remarkable individual including, but not limited to, thespian and musical vocalization abilities of a rare and high order.

## Summation of Characteristics

Dynamic illuminary in confident command of multitudinal talents of diverse and far-ranging nature as well as a strong sense of purpose and determination. Scholarly achievements while in attendance of highly reputable educational institutions were of a caliber seldom, if ever, exceeded. Full import of artistic gifts and abilities are yet to be recognized by the general American public although have proven readily apparent to a select group of writers, poets, musicians, etc., as well as the European theatre community as a result of the recent English tour.

## Educational Information

– *Columbia Law School, New York, New York • Law Degree, 1923*
– *Rutgers University, New Brunswick, New Jersey*
   *Honors Graduate (Four-Year Scholarship), 1919*
   – Captain of the Debating Society • Cap & Skull Honor Society
   – Phi Beta Kappa, Junior Year • 13 Varsity Letters (4 sports)
   – All-America Football Team, 1917 & 1918
   – Delivered Graduation Commencement Speech
– *Somerville High, Somerville, New Jersey • Graduate, 1915*
   – Greek, Latin, History, Literature, Philosophy, Physics
– *James L. Jamison's School, Somerville, New Jersey, 1910*

## Employment Information

• Various summer situations in Narragansett, Rhode Island, throughout school
• Professional Football Player, 1920

## Theatrical Productions to Date

• **Lead rôle**, *Simon The Cyrenian*, Harlem YMCA, New York, 1920
• **Lead rôle**, *Taboo*, (produced as *Voodoo* during English tour, Summer 1922)
• Provincetown Players Productions, James Light, Director: *All God's Chillun Got Wings*, May 1924 • *Emperor Jones*, July 1924

## Character References

• EUGENE O'NEILL (PLAYWRIGHT), PEAKED HILL BAR, PROVINCETOWN, MASS.
• JAMES LIGHT (DIRECTOR/STAGE MANAGER), MAISON CLEMENCEAU, 86 GREENWICH AVE., NEW YORK
• PABLO NERUDA (POET)

# Jackie Robinson
c/o 121 Pepper Street
Pasadena, California

**Objective**
A starting position with a Major League baseball team that would stand to benefit from the direct application of the proven & exceptional athletic abilities & talents of this extraordinary competitor. This appointment will surely prove to have lasting historical and sociological significance as well as offer bold new horizons to the Great American Pastime.

**Compact Biography**
An athletic marvel the likes of whom has not graced the American fields & courts of sport since the halcyon days of Red Grange and Jim Thorpe, to whom he is often rightfully compared, excelling, as he does, with great vigor & skill, at Football, Baseball, Basketball, Track & Field, Golf, and Tennis.

**Early Athletic Successes**

Washington Junior High School, Pasadena, California
Individual and Team Sports, 1933–1936
*John Muir Technical High School*, Pasadena; 1937 Graduate
- Letter Awards in Football, Basketball, Baseball, Track
- Selected for Pomona All-Star Baseball Team, 1937 (teammates included Ted Williams and Bob Lemon)
- Opponents' regularly stated strategy: "Stop Robinson!"

Pasadena Junior College, Pasadena, 1937–1939
- As Quarterback, led Pasadena to the Junior College Football Championship in 1938 with a record of 11 consecutive victories; gained over 1,000 yards from scrimmage and personally scored 131 of the team's 369 points All-Southern California Junior College shortstop (.417 average; 25 stolen bases in 24 games; 1938 MVP)
- All-State Basketball Team: Average 19 points per game
- NCAA National Junior College Broad Jump Champion
- Winner, Pacific Coast Intercollegiate Golf Championship
- Semifinalist, National Negro Tennis Tournament

University of California, Los Angeles, 1939–1941
- First 4-Letter Athlete in school's history
- Best runner in college football, 1939; average 12 yards per carry
- Led Southern Pacific Basketball Conference in scoring, 1939–1941
- National Collegiate Champion: Broad Jump

**Professional Sports**
- Los Angeles Bulldogs, 1941
- Honolulu Bears, 1941 (Returned to U.S. on the *Lurline*, 12/5/41)
- Kansas City Monarchs, 1945
- Scouted by Montreal Royals, Summer 1945

**Military History**
U.S. Army, 1942–1944; commissioned 2nd Lieutenant, 1943; Honorable Discharge, November 1944

# William Penn Adair "Will" Rogers

c/o Willie Hammerstein
Hammerstein's Roof Garden Vaudeville Theatre
New York, New York

---

## Situation Sought

Remunerative employment that will make use of natural talent for being able to make folks laugh and generally not take matters too seriously. Not necessarily seeking a position in politics, however.

## Encapsulated Profile Summary

Amiable, genial, well-liked young fellow possessed of a quick and ready wit, which traits readily endear him to friends, comrades, and associates. Work experience and education rather lack attributes usually considered desirable in modern Gotham, but optimistic disposition and eager willingness to tackle almost anything lend credence to employability. A position in public speaking would seem suitable.

## Background Information and Education

► Born November 4 (Election Day), 1879, at Oolagah, Rogers County, Indian Territory (later Claremore, Oklahoma, "Home of the Best Radium Water in the World"), on the Verdigris River, one mile below Spencer Creek. Record of Birth No. 2340, Authenticated Rolls of the Cherokee Nation.

► Attended various Cherokee Nation schools, including Willie Halsell College and Drumgoul, as well as Kemper Military Academy, Boonville, Missouri, 1897. Well versed in *McGuffey's Fourth Reader* and *Ray's Arithmetic*.

## Employment History

☆ ***Ranch Hand***, Ewings Ranch, Higgins, Texas, 1898
☆ ***Owner***, Dog Iron Ranch, Oklahoma, 1899
☆ ***Buckaroo***, Col. Zack Mulhall, St. Louis Fair, 1899
☆ ***Drover***, Cattle Rancho, Argentina, South America, 1902
☆ ***Rough Rider & Lasso Thrower (The Cherokee Kid)***, Texas Jack's Wild West Show, Johannesburg, South Africa, 1902–1903
☆ **Mexican Rope Artist**, Wirth Bros. Circus, Sydney, Australia, 1903
☆ **All-Around Rider**, Cummings & Mulhall Wild West Show on the Pike, 1904
☆ **Extra Act (Lariat Thrower)**, Hammerstein's Roof Garden, New York, 1905

## Acclamation

*"The Cherokee Kid has performed with me during my present South African tour and I consider him to be the champion trick Rough Rider and Lasso Thrower in the world. He is sober, industrious, hard working at all times and is always to be relied upon. I shall be pleased to give him an engagement at any time should he wish to return."*

—Texas Jack

### First Man in the World to Lasso a Wild Zebra!

# Damon Runyon

320 West 102nd Street
New York, New York

## Situation Sought

A soft and profitable dodge, perhaps artichokes or extortion, which will be sure to line the pockets of the guy with an enormous amount of potatoes indeed, but will not have anything to do with a normal 9-to-5'er, as before such a guy would have any truck with the likes of that he would as soon place his noggin in a fire, or maybe sooner.

## Bio-Scape

- A scribe of no mean standing among this burg's big guys and ever-loving dolls.
- Not an old guy, but you can get plenty of 8-to-5 that he is shoving on toward 40 these days.
- Well known and celebrated in the speaks and joints along the Hardened Artery called Broadway, where his word is his bond.
- Reliable in a pinch, and known to chuck quite a swell from time to time, although always sober as a Shiite.
- Recommends floating a finnif on Pharaoh's Folly in the 4th at Pimlico.

## Background

▶ Joined the 13th Minnesota Volunteers at the age of 14 to fight the Spanish in the Philippines and sailed with the first American expeditionary force to ever leave the Western Hemisphere, 1898. Contributed articles to various magazines including the *Manila Freedom*, the *Soldier's Letter*, and the *Souvenir Song Book*; wounded at the Battle of Inmus and the Battle of Samar; mustered out, November 1899

▶ *Reporter*, the *Pueblo Chieftain*, 1900–1902

▶ Various journalistic situations, 1902–1906; in San Francisco for the Big Earthquake, April 1906.

▶ *Reporter*, *Denver News, Denver Republican, Denver Post*, 1907–1908

▶ First trip to New York, 1908, to cover the Electric Light Utility Worker's Convention

▶ *Sports Columnist*, *San Francisco Post*, 1908; coined Jack Dempsey's "Manassa Mauler" handle

▶ *Sportswriter/Reporter*, *New York American*. Assignments included:
• Mexican revolution coverage, 1912 • New York Giants • Chicago White Sox Round the World Tour, 1913 (reported from London) • Correspondent with General "Blackjack" Pershing's Mexican campaign, 1916 • European War Correspondent with the 1st Army at Argonne and Meuse and with Major General Omar Bundy's 2nd Division at Vaux, 1917 • Started "Both Barrels," sports column for Hearst's International News Service, 1918 • Covered Democratic National Convention, San Francisco, 1920

## References

None necessary. Read his stuff.

# Harland Sanders

Sanders Court & Cafe
Junction U.S. Highways 25, 25E, & 25W
Corbin, Laurel County, Kentucky

## Statement of Intent

To develop, perfect, and promote a revolutionary new method of cooking chicken that will consistently offer a top-quality dining experience by establishing singularly high standards of taste, flavor, savoriness, and palatability unprecedented in the restaurant industry. Eventual expansion outside the State of Kentucky is anticipated, don't you see.

## Brief Biographical Recapitulation

- Independent, hard-driven, strong-willed, and somewhat of a stickler concerning quality of the product.
- Exceptionally wide and diverse employment background has led to a thorough understanding of effective methods of business operation.
- Reputed to possess a bit of a temper, but ambiguous reports of throwing fried eggs at cooks have never been substantiated.

## History of Employments

• Farmhand, 1900–1901, Henryville & New Albany, Indiana • Fare Collector, 1904–1905, New Albany Street Car Company • U.S. Army, Cuban Tour, 1905 • Blacksmith's Helper/Fireman, 1906–1910, Southern R.R. • Fireman/Section Hand, 1911–1914, Western, Illinois Central, and Rock Island Line R.R.

### 1915–1930:

• Self-employed Legalist • Insurance Salesman/Assistant Supervisor, Prudential Life Insurance Company • Salesman, Mutual Benefit Life of New Jersey • Stockbroker, New Albany–Louisville Ferryboat Co. • Executive Secretary, Columbus, Indiana, Chamber of Commerce • Acetylene Lamp Manufacturer • Salesman, Michelin Tire Company of Louisville • Filling Station Operator, Standard Oil of Kentucky

## Synopsis of Recently Devised Recipe Preparation
## Methods & Experimentations

► Trial & error testing of the "pressure cooker," an innovative new cooking device
► Inquiries concerning proper temperature of the cooking oil & cooking time
► Exploratory experiments concerning whether to pre-fry and, if so, for how long
► Techniques to prevent the drying out of the chicken & preserving the texture
► Kitchen testing of specially mixed flours and proper wash techniques
► Development, revision, and perfection of proper blends of suitable herbs & spices

*• President, Kentucky Restaurant Association • Member, National Restaurant Association • Former District Supervisor, Works Progress Administration • Commissioned Kentucky Colonel (Ruby Laffoon, Governor) • Listed in "Adventures in Good Eating," Duncan Hines, Editor, 1939*

# I G N A Z   S C H W I N N

ARNOLD, SCHWINN & COMPANY
PEORIA AND LAKE STREETS
CHICAGO, ILLINOIS

---

## Proclamation of Intent

To announce to the Bicycling Public the development of innovative new devices, designs, developments, and accessories that are sure to prove to be beneficial to the enjoyment of the pastime, as well as enhance the superior mode of transportation offered by the bicycle.

## A Brief Delineation of the Firm

Incorporated by the Principal and his associate in Chicago in October 1895, a time when there were upwards of 300 bicycle companies in the Nation, the company was formed to manufacture and sell bicycles, sulkies, wagons, carrioles, and sundry conveyances, and at once, in great earnest, began establishing an unexcelled reputation for unsurpassed mechanical ingenuity, excellence in engineering, and innovative styling. The Standard Roadster (Model 22) and the companion Ladies' Model were the first examples introduced to a grateful public, and they established a foundation of quality & reliability that endures to this day, proudly carrying on the Grand Tradition established by these machines:

◉ The "Celerifere" (1790) ◉ The "Draisienne," or "Hobby Horse" (1816) ◉ The "MacMillan" (1839) ◉ The "Velocipede," or "Boneshaker" (1863) ◉ The "Ordinary," or "High Wheeler" (1870) ◉ The "Triocycle," or "Jolly Boat for 3 persons" (1880) ◉ The "Safety" (1884)

## Recent Progresses & Advances in Manufacture

◉ The Autocycle—Greater Beauty, Greater Comfort, Greater Safety—1936
◉ The Cycleplane for 1935 (Model 35 and Model 35 De Luxe)
◉ The Streamline Aerocycle—Strikingly New & Modern for 1934

### AND

### (in production or anticipated):

◉ Super Balloon Tires on the Deep Drop Center Rim ◉ The Cyclelock ◉ Theft-Proof, Tamper Proof, Fool-Proof ◉ Full-Floating Saddle ◉ "Stimsonite" Rear Reflector ◉ Fore-Wheel & Expander Brakes ◉ Knee-Action Spring Fork ◉ Cantilever Truss Frame ◉ Fender Light

## Significant Milestones in the History of the Company

- 1899: Riding a Schwinn machine, Mile-a-Minute Murphy becomes the first man to travel 60 mph.
- 1900–1910: Triumphs of the World Racing Team include numerous record-breaking victories in individual categories, paced racing (utilizing triplets, quads, and quintets), and 6-day marathon racing.
- 1911: Arnold, Schwinn & Co. absorbs the Excelsior Motor Cycle Company; 1917: The Henderson Motor Cycle Company is purchased.
- 1896–1905: Four experimental motor cars are built at the factory.
- 1917–1918: Significant contributions are made by the Company to war materials production.

*New designs currently in the planning stages include the "Hollywood" for Ladies, the "Cycle Truck," the Improved "Autocycle Deluxe," the "Superior," and the "Paramount."*

## "FOR MEN MAY COME, AND MEN MAY GO, BUT WE ROLL ON FOREVER."

# SITTING BULL

## (Tatanka Iyotake)
### c/o Mrs. Catherine Weldon
### Standing Rock Agency, Dakota Territory

## Proclamation of Ultimate Intent

The purpose of the great Hunkpapa *Itanchan* (Chief of Chiefs) is twofold: First, to elevate the status and condition of the Sioux people to their rightful and proper station in modern American life, and secondly, to educate and enlighten white Americans in all matters concerning true Indian ways and ideals.

## Concise Biographical Compendium

Born in the early 1830s on the Grand River in Dakota Territory and given the boyhood name *Hunk-es-ni* (Slow). Killed first buffalo at the age of 10 and became a warrior at 14 by counting coup on a Crow enemy in battle. Brief summation of history as warrior and war chief follows:

➤ Membership in the Strong Heart Warrior Society, 1857
➤ Chief of Northern Sioux, 1866; chosen as *Itanchan*, 1867
➤ Negotiated the Treaty of Laramie, 1867
➤ Leader of War Council (Sioux, Arapaho, Cheyenne), 1875
➤ Whipped Lt. Col. George A. Custer and the 7th Cavalry at the Greasy Grass (Little Big Horn), June 25, 1876
➤ Surrendered 1881, imprisoned at Fort Randall for two years; released to Standing Rock Agency, 1883

## Further Background Information

● Attended, in the company of General Grant and other dignitaries, the ceremony of the laying of the cornerstone of the Dakota capital at Bismarck, 1883
● Toured the Eastern U.S. for purposes of education and instruction under the auspices of Col. Alvaren Allen of St. Paul, September–October 1884. Engagements included:
  • Minnesota Agricultural Fair • Eden Musée, New York • Music Hall, Brooklyn
● Joined Buffalo Bill Cody's Wild West Show & Congress of Rough Riders, June 1885. Toured the United States and Canada, June–October 1885

## Clarifications

The Chief wishes it known and understood that there are matters concerning his history that have been misrepresented to a certain degree among the general population. It is his desire to set the record straight as concerns them.

1. Sitting Bull is not a half-French graduate of West Point Military Academy.

2. He did not write and publish "The Works of Sitting Bull," a collection of French and Latin language poems published in 1878.

3. The Sioux language does not easily lend itself to literal translation into English. As a result, certain concepts lose their true meaning when translated from the Indian tongue. The popular name of the Chief is an example of this. A fuller understanding of his stature among his people can be achieved through the contemplation of the accurate rendering of his name:

## THE WISE ONE WHO HAS COME TO BE AMONG US

# JEDEDIAH STRONG SMITH

**c/o Postmaster**
**Independence, Missouri**

## Statement of Intent

Seeking to strike an Agreement with a benevolent Patron concerning sponsorship of a Proposed Expedition to explore and map a new and expeditious Trade Route through the Cut-Off into the New Mexican Territory of Santa Fé.

## Syllabus of Accomplishments

By mutual consent of all men involved in the Fur Trade the most thoroughly skilled and experienced Mountain Man surviving to this day. More than a Decade spent engaged in the exploration of the Trackless Wilds of the Western Wilderness while hunting and trapping the Beaver. Veteran of Homeric Odysseys of Epic Proportions involving laborious, dangerous exposures and privations that have served to develop a pronounced ability to endure & survive Monstrous Hardships and all manner of Precarious Endeavors. Numerous encounters with various Tribes of Hostile Savages have evolved the Partisan into an unparalleled Journeyman Indian Fighter.

## A Brief Biographical Historiette

◎ Born in Bainbridge, Chenago County, New York State, 1798 ◎

◎ A fair English education, some Latin; possesses the ability to write a good hand ◎

◎ Served as Clerk aboard a Lake Erie freighter, 1811 ◎

◎ First journey West: 1818 ◎

## Journeys & Peregrinations in the Fur Trade, and Extended Intrepid Explorations

◎ Member of the William H. Ashley & Andrew Henry Rocky Mountain venture, 1822

◎ Ascended the Missouri River region in the employ of Ashley & Henry, 1823

◎ Rediscovered the South Pass while engaged in a trapping expedition, 1824

◎ Purchased William Ashley's trading interests and led party from the Great Salt Lake through the Mojave Desert into the California Territory; explored San Gabriel and areas north; returned to Salt Lake through the Sierra Nevada and the desert of the Great Basin. First White Man to enter Alta California from the East and return overland, 1826–1827

◎ Repeated the journey soon after return, but suffered the loss of the majority of the party at the hands of Mojave Indians. Traveled the length of California and explored the Coast of Oregon, where all but two of the surviving trappers were slain by Umpqua Indians; explorations opened the coastal route from California to Fort Vancouver on the Columbia River, 1827–1828

THE PARTISAN PROPOSES TO EMBARK ON THE SANTA FÉ EXPEDITION
AT THE ONSET OF THE SUMMER—
FOR PARTICULARS INQUIRE OF THE SUBSCRIBER
OR THE CLERK OF WORKS,
ROCKY MOUNTAIN FUR COMPANY.

# Gertrude Stein

*27 RUE DE FLEURUS*
PARIS, FRANCE

### TO STATE INTENT IS INTENTION OF THE STATEMENT

To travel to America yes our America. We in our ship. Our ship *Champlain* traveling to America traveling *aller et retour* from Le Havre to New York we sail strange but my gracious yes strange we are lions and celebrities traveling to lecture to celebrate the tour to be, to be a tour triumphant.

### APERÇU

The monolithic, coy, shrewd, and eccentric Matron Saint of Paris Art has produced a very wide body of important work considered by many to be the literary counterpart of cubism and abstraction, and the direct descendant of the stream of consciousness techniques & empirical procedure theories of William James. Prolific, avant-garde creator of plays, portraits, poems, cameos, illuminations, and often incomprehensible prose, the Sibyl of Montparnesse is renowned by the *literati* of the Continent for spontaneous automatic writing xperiments, a pure passion for xactitude, and xploring the realms of the "continuous present," the "immediate existing," and the "including everything."

### PRINCIPAL PUBLICATIONS

- *Three Lives*, 1909
- *Geography and Plays*, 1922
- *Composition as Explanation*, 1926
- *Lucy Church Amiably*, 1927
- *Matisse, Picasso and Gertrude Stein*, 1933
- *The Autobiography of Alice B. Toklas*, 1932
- *Tender Buttons*, 1914
- *The Making of Americans*, 1925
- *Useful Knowledge*, 1928
- *How to Write*, 1931
- *Operas and Plays*, 1932
- *Portraits and Prayers*, 1934

### ART COLLECTION

*Personal collection includes original works of:*

- Cézanne
- Manet
- Rousseau
- Picasso
- Renoir
- Matisse
- Derain
- Gris
- Daumier
- Braque
- Gauguin
- Man Ray

### FORMAL EDUCATION

- A.B. (*magna cum laude*), Radcliffe College (Harvard Annex), 1898
- Johns Hopkins University Medical School, Baltimore, 1897–1901
- Oakland High School, Oakland, California (one year)

PRINCIPAL LITERARY/EDUCATIONAL INFLUENCES, IN ADDITION TO WM. JAMES, INCLUDE SHAKESPEARE, WORDSWORTH, BURNS, SMOLLETT, FIELDING, CARLYLE, SCOTT, SANTAYANA

### COPAINS AND CONSOCIATES

• F. Scott & Zelda Fitzgerald • Ezra Pound • Wyndham Lewis • André Gide • Sherwood Anderson • John Dos Passos • Paul Robeson • John Reed • Ford Madox Ford • Edith Sitwell • Carl Van Vechten • Thornton Wilder • Mabel Dodge • Jo Davidson • And all of the more significant contemporary French and Spanish painters

# LEVI STRAUSS

c/o Levi Strauss & Co.
14–16 Battery Street
San Francisco, California

## Proclamation of Purpose and Intent

To make application for and to secure, in conjunction with a business partner, a United States Patent to protect the improved new designs of riveted and reinforced waist overalls and pantaloons.

## Prospectus of the Enterprise and Elaboration of the Habiliment

A sturdy and durable article of attire designed specifically to withstand the rigors of everyday life in the mines, lumber camps, and roughshod towns of the West. Noteworthy facts concerning manufacturing details include:

✪ Currently being constructed of 10 oz. duck twill or 9 oz. denim. They are manufactured of the Best Material, and in a Superior Manner. A trial will convince everybody of this fact.

✪ Experimentation now being conducted regarding color variances and the practicality of adding blanket insulation for winter use.

✪ Proven popularity of riveting technique indicated by brisk sales of the pantaloons in Reno (200 pair sold from January 1871 to June 1872).

✪ Expansion of production to include vests, coats, jumpers, and blouses is anticipated.

✪ Adequate means of manufacture, supply, and distribution is assured; purchase of the Pacific Woolen Mills, oldest mills on the Pacific Coast, is expected.

## A Brief Syllabus of the Firm & Biographical Sketch of the Founder

The Company can accurately trace its origins to the year 1850, by which time the Gentleman, Mr. Levi Strauss, had established a successful enterprise as a traveling pack peddler based in New York City, having emigrated from Bavaria and settled in Gotham in the summer of 1847. San Francisco was reached in March of 1853, and a prosperous dry goods enterprise established there forthwith. Substantial levels of growth and prosperity have been achieved in the last 20 years, and the Levi Strauss Company stands now on the threshold of a bright and optimistic future.

*As an indication of the stability of Levi Strauss & Co., it should be noted that the firm prospered during the crises of the collapse of the Adams & Co. bank in 1855, the national panic of 1857, the years of the War Between the States, and the San Francisco earthquake of 1868.*

*• Member, Eureka Benevolent Society • Member, Reform Temple of Emanu-El*

## Business References & Testimonials

• Leland Stanford • Mark Hopkins • Domingo Ghiardelli • Jesse Seligman
• Issac Friedlander • James Ben Ali-Haggin • William Ralston

# Billy Sunday

1111 Sunday Lane
Winona Lake, Indiana

### Divinely Ordained Purpose & Mission

To march triumphant on the sawdust trail into New York City, the infamous, godforsaken, hell-bound Sodom that smites the sacred, City of scoffers and sin-stained cynics, ever dodging the missiles of Satan's dirty imps & marksmen while bringing the Good Word of Jesus Christ's Glorious Testament of Purity, Sobriety, and Righteousness, drenched in tears of repentance, to the Legions of the hell-soaked drunkards, purveyors of godless ideology, bull-neck degenerates, and ungathered masses of the unsaved.

### Conspectus of the Revival to Save New York

God's Greatest Grenadier will spread the fiery Word of the Great Umpire of the Universe at the Glory Barn in Washington Heights at the corner of 168th Street & Broadway beginning April 18 and continuing until the myriads of trailhitters fill the upbound Gospel Train of the Heavenly Procession soon to embark on the straight and narrow track on a nonstop homeward journey to the Glorious & Everlasting Depot of Eternal Salvation.

### Historiette of Evangelical Successes

♦ Over 60 jay-rube burg midwestern tent revivals, 1895–1900
♦ First tabernacle revival, Perry, Iowa, 1901 (Seating: 1,000)
♦ Average populations of cities visited: 1907: 10,000; 1908: 20,000; 1913: 76,000; 1914: 171,000; 1916: 584,000 ➜20 different states: 1908–1917 ➜ First N.Y. Revival, 1914
♦ Representative Headlines: "PREACHER SETS TOWN AFIRE" • "EVANGELIST DOES GREAT STUNTS IN TABERNACLE PULPIT" • "SUNDAY A WHIRLWIND" • "SUNDAY A GREAT DAY" • "THIS IS 'BIG BUSINESS' FOR THE LORD" • "A DRY MANHATTAN BILLY'S FONDEST HOPE" • "SUNDAY FLAYS BAD MOTHERS" • "SUNDAY AND THE FLAG GIVE CROWD A THRILL"

### Sermons

♦ *Booze, or Get on the Water Wagon*
♦ *And He Said, "Tomorrow"*
♦ *The Sins of Society*
♦ *Hot Cakes Off the Griddle*
♦ *Earnestness in Christian Life*

♦ *Have Ye Received the Holy Spirit?*
♦ *Moral Lepers*
♦ *The Forces That Win*
♦ *How to Be a Man*
♦ *No Second Chance*

### Concise Personal Compendium

•"The Fastest Man In Baseball," Chicago White Stockings, 1883–1891 • Ass't. Secretary (Religious Dept.), Chicago YMCA, 1891–1893 • Advance Man/General Factotum, J. William Chapman's Revivals, 1893–1895 • Religious Studies, Evanston Academy, 1887–1888 • Converted to Christ, Pacific Garden Mission, Chicago, 1886 • Bible Studies, Chicago YMCA, 1889–1890 • Ordained 1903, Chicago Presbytery • "Eighth Greatest Man in the United States" —*American Magazine* poll, 1914

### Significant Personages Influenced by the Word

• John D. Rockefeller • William Jennings Bryan • John M. Studebaker • Henry Clay Frick • S. S. Kresge • Theodore Roosevelt • Louis F. Swift

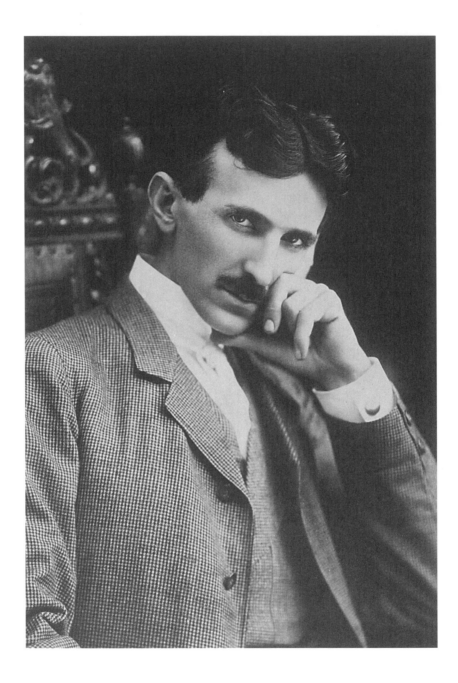

# Nikola Tesla
c/o Bailey Cottage, Wardencliff
Long Island, New York

## Prospective Purpose & Intention

To secure all necessary sponsorship and financial support regarding the development, construction, and implementation of the World Wireless Power & Broadcasting Center on Long Island, which is currently being designed to transmit both high voltage electric power and communications anywhere on the Globe wirelessly as well as fulfill the present need of providing an efficient method of illumination to the populace.

## Operational Synopsis, or What It Will Do

✢ Send voice messages, signals, and other communications instantaneously to any point on Earth utilizing receivers no larger than a pocket watch. The wireless transmission of visual images is a distinct possibility in the future, as well.

✢ Transmit electrical power, by use of the Earth itself as a conductor, anywhere in the world without the use of wire, thereby annihilating the constraints of distance.

✢ Allow telephone subscribers to talk to one another, anywhere, anytime, with only the use of compact handheld transmitters/receivers.

✢ Accurate facsimile transmission of documents, letters, handwritten characters, photographic images, drawings, etc.

✢ Interconnection and universal operation of all the world's stock tickers.

✢ Universal establishment of navigation systems to enable all ships at sea to steer perfectly without the aid of the compass and to pinpoint location, course, and destination, as well as detect the presence of other vessels from great distances.

✢ Worldwide coordination and standardization of economically feasible timekeeping methods.

## Educational Vitae

■ Normal School, Smiljan, Lika Province, Yugoslavia, 1866 ■ Real Gymnasium, Gospic, 1866–1870 ■ Higher Real Schule, Karlovac, 1870–1873 ■ Polytechnic School, Gratz, 1875–1878 (First Alternating Current Experiments) ■ University of Prague (Physics) and Buda-Pesth (Languages), 1880–1881

## Vocational Stations

■ Assistant Engineer, Government Telegraph Engineering Department, Buda-Pesth, 1881
■ Electrical Engineer, Continental Edison Company, Paris, France, 1882–1883
■ Research Engineer, The Edison Industrial-Research Works, Pearl Street, New York, 1884–1885
■ Founder, Tesla Electric Company, So. Fifth Ave., New York

## Accomplishments, Inventions, & Discoveries

• Alternating Current Induction Motor • Tesla Coil • Rotating Magnetic Field • 3 Phase Power Systems • Lighting System, World Columbian Exposition, Chicago, 1893 • AC Generating System, Niagara Falls Hydroelectric Station • Wireless Arc Lighting • Teleautomatics • Radio-Control • Principles of Radio

## Testimonials Available From:

• J. Pierpont Morgan, Financier • Stanford White, Architect • Mark Twain, Author
• George Westinghouse, Industrialist • A. K. Brown, Western Union • J. S. Warden, Suffolk Land Co.

# JIM THORPE
704 East Boston Street
Yale, Oklahoma

## PURPOSE & INTENT

To petition the International Olympic Committee, the American Olympic Committee, the Swedish Olympic Committee, and the Amateur Athletic Union to reinstate to Mr. Thorpe the Gold Medals won at the 1912 Olympics that he was forced to return after it became public knowledge that he had received payment as a professional baseball player (1909–1911).

## CONCISE SUMMATION

*Unquestionably the greatest all-around athlete of the young century, Jim Thorpe created an endless wellspring of public emotion & patriotism by soundly trouncing all competition in the Pentathlon & Decathlon events at the 1912 Olympics in Stockholm. Countless legions of admirers and followers do hereby protest the aforementioned organizations' decision to deny him the honors, and respectfully & formally demand their return, forthwith and with all due haste.*

## OLYMPIC TRIUMPHS

### GOLD MEDALS, Pentathlon & Decathlon, 1912, Stockholm

- Broad Jump: 23' 2$\frac{7}{10}$"
- High Hurdles: 15$\frac{6}{10}$ seconds
- Javelin: 153' 2$\frac{19}{20}$"
- Discus: 116' 8$\frac{4}{10}$"
- High Jump: 6' 1$\frac{6}{10}$"
- Shot Put: 42' 5$\frac{9}{20}$"
- 1,500 Meter Race: 4 minutes 40.1 seconds
- Total Decathlon points: 8,412.955

## BIOGRAPHY

- Born May 28, 1888, in Prague, Oklahoma, named in the Sac and Fox language Wa-tho-huck (Bright Path), a direct descendant of the great chief Black Hawk
- Enrolled at Haskell Indian Junior College, Lawrence, Kansas, 1898
- Entered Carlisle Indian Academy, Carlisle, Pennsylvania, 1904, and excelled at all athletics
- 1912 track season victories include the Boston, Pittsburgh, and Middle Athletic Associations and the Carnegie Meet
- Married Iva Miller, 1913, embarked on world tour honeymoon, and returned to U.S. aboard the *Lusitania*

## PROFESSIONAL SPORTS HISTORY TO DATE

**BASEBALL, 1913–1919:** New York Giants, Cincinnati Reds, Boston Braves
**1909–1911:** East Carolina League. Lifetime major league batting average: .252
**FOOTBALL, 1915–Present:** Canton Bulldogs, Rock Island Independents, New York Giants, Oorang Indians (Elected President of the American Professional Football Association, 1920)

## TESTIMONIALS IN SUPPORT OF RETURN OF THE MEDALS

Provided by the *Philadelphia Times, Buffalo Enquirer, London Pall Mall Gazette, London Daily News,* and the *Toronto Mail and Empire* ("Canadians Stand Firm With Our Jim Thorpe. Canada Has Declared For Jim Thorpe"), as well as from notable sports personages Glenn Scobey "Pop" Warner and sportswriter Damon Runyon.

# James Thurber

c/o 25 West 45th Street
New York, New York

## Prospective Volition

To be busted, demoted, and reduced (with salary increased accordingly) from current situation as ersatz Managing Editor, or "hand-holder" of artists, of struggling, yet promising, cosmopolitan magazine, and to secure an ultimately more prestigious position as writer of nonsense casuals, parodies, formula stuff, etc., for same.

## Predicaments, Perplexities, Sum & Substance

Recently returned from Paris, a sojourn characterized by an acute lack of francs, not meeting Fitzgerald or Hemingway, and not publishing a novel. A preoccupation with the smaller enormities of life, pronounced lack of high seriousness, and campaign against carcinomenclature has led to, at best, sketchy employment in the field of journalism, a fine quandary. Familiar with the phenomenon of having articles and submissions returned like tennis serves, it is high time the partially unreconstructed midwesterner abandoned all appearances of the sophisticated cosmopolite and quit guessing at what tomorrow may bring.

## Past Life & Hard Times

### JOURNALISTIC ENDEAVORS:

❖ "Why We Behave Like Microbe Hunters" (yet to be published) ❖ Reporter, *New York Evening Post*, 1926 ❖ "Josephine Has Her Day" (short story), 1926 ❖ Various overseas observations published in the *New York World, New York Herald, Kansas City Star, Detroit Athletic Club News*, etc., 1925 ❖ Reporter, Paris & Riviera Editions, *Chicago Tribune*, 1925 ❖ "A Sock on the Jaw—French Style," *Harper's*, 1925 ❖ Central Ohio Correspondent, *The Christian Science Monitor*, 1924 ❖ Contributor, *Wheeling Intelligencer*, 1924 ❖ "Credos and Curios," Sunday half-page column, *Columbus Dispatch*, 1923 (42 columns) ❖ Reporter, *Dispatch*, 1921–22 ❖ Interviews: Thomas A. Edison, Gen. Pershing, Rudolph Valentino, Isadora Duncan, Mrs. Harry Houdini

### OTHER EMPLOYMENT:

**Code Clerk**, U.S. State Department, Washington, D.C., & Paris, November 1918–March 1920

### SCHOOLING:

#### Ohio State University, Columbus, Ohio, 1913–1918

- Phi Kappa Psi
- Contributor, the *Ohio State Lantern*
- Editor-In-Chief, the *Sun Dial*
- Member, the Strollers Theatrical Club

**Musical Comedies written & directed with the Scarlet Mask Club of OSU, 1921–1925:**
*Oh My, Omar; Psychomania; Many Moons; A Twin Fix; The Cat and the Riddle*

## References & Testimonials

- J. Wesley Millmoss • Mr. Sealyham • Messr. Webley-Vickers • Mrs. Ulgine Barrows
- Pearl du Monville • Lt. Col. H. R. L. Le Boutelier, C.I.E.

# B. Traven

c/o Dobbs Literary Agency
New York, New York

**Objective**    Publication of works of fiction (novels).

**Profile**    Reclusive individual of mysterious, nebulous background. Little was revealed to the interviewer concerning subject's personal history, although it is asserted by various reliable sources that his lineage is that of certain European royalty, which claim is somewhat substantiated in the style, dialogue, and idiom of his prose.

**Education**    No information.

**Military Service**    No record.

**Employment History**    Unknown.

**Marital Status**    Believed married.

**Residence**    Reported to maintain residence in Mexico.

**Works in Progress**

- A powerful, gripping, savage attack on the foibles of capitalism and the eternal struggle of the working class set aboard a doomed, desperate freighter sailing the Atlantic and Mediterranean.
- A masterful revelation of human nature and searing discourse on the folly of greed personified in the tale of three gold seekers struggling after a paydirt strike in the wilds of Mexico's Sierra Madre range.

*Aforementioned works previously published in Germany.*

*No testimonials or references available.*

# HARRIET TUBMAN

180 South Street, Auburn, New York

**Purpose & Intent**

To secure for Mrs. Tubman the federal pension she is entitled to for the provision of heroic & exemplary services to the Union Army during the War Between the States.

**Biographical Vignette**

Dedicated and devoted leader of the Abolitionist cause, she personally guided over 300 escaped slaves to safety in the North by way of the Underground Railroad. During the late war, she served the Union cause with great distinction, her courage, dedication, and fortitude attested to by numerous Army officers and statesmen.

**History**

- Born into slavery (as Araminta Ross) ca. 1820, Dorchester County, Maryland
- Owned by Edward Broda; rented at different times to James Cook, John Stewart, and Dr. Anthony Thompson
- Married James Tubman, 1844
- Fled Broda plantation, 1849
- Conducted escapes through the Underground Railroad, 1850–1860; rewards posted by slave owners for her capture totaled $60,000 by 1860; by and by led her aged parents to freedom
- Performed meritorious service as Spy, Scout, Cook, and Nurse for the Union Army, 1862–1865, including participation in the Port Royal raid on the Combahee River of June 2, 1863, with Colonel James Montgomery's 1st Detachment, 2nd South Carolina Volunteers

**Testimonials & Publications**

Upheld and championed by all Abolitionist publications, including:
- *The Liberator*
- *The North Star*
- *Freedom's Journal*
- *The National Anti-Slavery Standard*
- *Genius of Universal Emancipation*

Works written and published on her behalf by Mrs. Sarah Hopkins Bradford with the generous assistance of Gerrit Smith and Wendell Phillips are:

–*Scenes in the Life of Harriet Tubman*, 1869

–*Harriet, The Moses of Her People*, Revised, 1886

**References**

- Frederick W. Seward of Montrose-on-Hudson, N.Y., son of the late Secretary of State
- William Lloyd Garrison, Publisher • Frederick Douglass, Rochester, N.Y. • Ezekiel Hunn, William Still, and Thomas Garrett, Abolitionists and Underground Railroad Conductors

# Wells, Fargo & Co.

Parrott Building
California & Montgomery Streets
San Francisco, California

## PUBLIC NOTICE OF INTENT TO ENGAGE SERVICES

Seeking to enlist, enroll, or otherwise retain the deputation & services of Stalwart, Dauntless, & Intrepid Lawmen in an Earnest Effort to curtail and foil the Plague of Robberies, Brigandages, and Depredations being perpetrated on Company Stagecoaches transporting GOLD BULLION, SPECIE, & DUST throughout Alta California.

## CONCISE PROSPECTUS
## OF THE WELLS, FARGO CONSORTIUM

*"Transportation of Gold Our Specialty—Always in a Secure & Timely Manner"*
*"Any and All Losses Promptly Reimbursed, in Full, to the Shipper"*

■ Wells, Fargo & Co., Express & Banking, Incorporated March 18, 1852
■ Capital Stock Increased to $2,000,000 by 1865
■ Absorbed Holladay Overland Mail Company, 1866
■ Transported $58,000,000 in Gold Bullion over California Roads in 1858
■ HENRY WELLS, FINANCIAL OFFICER; WILLIAM G. FARGO, OPERATIONS SUPERINTENDENT

### A Census of the Bold Jehus, the Gallant Stagedrivers, the Fearless Knights of the Western Lash Whose Protection Must Be Ensured...

• Hank Monk • Curly Dan Burch • Charlie Carroll • Ned Blair
• Coon Hollow Charlie • Uncle Jimmy Miller • Pop McCray
• Jared Crandall • Jim Stewart (The Silent Terror)

### ...To Better Serve These Never Idle Interior Mining Camps...

• Fiddletown • Sonora • Marysville • Quincy • Hangtown • Oroville • Ione • Chinese Camp
• Mokelumne Hill • Columbia • Downieville • Yankee Camp • Tuttletown • Dutch Flat
• Soldier's Gulch • Angel's Camp • El Dorado • Coloma • Half-Oz Gulch
• Jesus Maria • Calaveras Crossing • Murphy's Camp • Bay State Ranch

### ...and to Safeguard Same from the Onslaught of Foul & Pestiferous Depredations That Have Been Perpetrated on Them by a Heinous Company of Scurrilous & Infamous Blackguards, viz.:

• "Rattlesnake Dick" Barter • Reelfoot William's Gang • Tom Bell's Bunch
• "Kentucky" Watkins • R. Henry Ingram • Mickey Free • Pedro Pablo • White Rock Jack
• Lazarus (O-Lan-O) • Indian Dick • Bill Early • El Macho • Louis Dreibelbis

## DARING DESPERADOES ALL!

*Interested Parties Should Immediately Contact an Agent of Wells, Fargo & Co., or Make Direct Application to the Principals at the Above Address. Unmarried Men & Veterans of the War Between the States Preferred.*

# James McNeill Whistler

**The White House in Tite Street**
**Chelsea, London, England**

---

## Ultimate Animus & Intention

To enlist popular support in America regarding the current legal proceedings instituted by the Artist in answer to the scurrilous, heinous, and vexatious libel precipitated by an inept baboon of an ersatz English art critic, the slanderous blather and drivel of whom reflects, with malicious negativism, on both the integrity of the Artist and the American people as a whole.

## Personified Capitulation

Painter of the Night, Painter of the Sea, Painter of the Poetry of Sight, master of line, style, form, and composition; cosmopolitan, urbane, and the personification of wit, cheer, & raillery; the Bohemian of the Bohemians & "always on the wing," he was born, by choice, in St. Petersburg, Russia, or in Baltimore, Maryland, or, if need be, in Lowell, Massachusetts, and has maintained continuous residence in Europe for the past 23 years, expatriated, but "shall come to America when the duty on works of art is abolished!"

## Refutations & Rebuttals of Criticisms

❈ **Item:** How, asks a critic, can a price of 200 guineas be placed on a work of art that was two days in the making? The answer is that it is not the price of the individual painting that is at issue, rather that the cost is determined by placing a monetary value on the interpretive and technical knowledge attained throughout a lifetime.

❈ **Item:** That critics take exception to the choice of the artist's mother as the subject of one of his most brilliant works when the true subject of study and appreciation should be, as the name of the painting implies, an "Arrangement in Gray and Black."

❈ **Item:** An especially tiresome, wooden-headed, and insipid self-professed "critic" finds fault with the use of any and all color in a work entitled "Symphony in White No. III", thereby leading the public to believe that he would expect a musical piece written in the key of F to be simply a repetition of F-F-F-F-F. Stupidity Redefined! Bon Dieu!

## Representative Epitome of Artistic Achievements to Date

❈ *The White Girl (Symphony in White #1)* ❈ *Coast of Brittany* ❈ *Last of Old Westminster* ❈ *At the Piano* ❈ *Little White Girl* ❈ *Portrait of Thomas Carlyle* ❈ *Miss Cicely Alexander* ❈ *Japonaiserie: Caprice in Purple and Gold* ❈ *Gold Girl* ❈ *Yellow Buskin* ❈ *Arrangement in Gray and Black* ❈ *Nocturne in Black and Gold: The Falling Rocket* ❈ *The Thames in Ice*

## Confreres, Consociates, Colleagues, & Cronies

• GEORGE DU MAURIER • IGNACE FANTIN-LATOUR • ALPHONSE LEGROS • OSCAR WILDE • EDGAR DEGAS • EDOUARD MANET • GUSTAVE COURBET • FRANÇOIS ST. BONVIN • DANTE GABRIEL ROSSETTI • ALGERNON CHARLES SWINBURNE • SEYMOUR HADEN, PATRON • FREDERICK LEYLAND, PATRON

Exhibitions held at Grosvenor Gallery, London, & Salon des Refusés, Paris, among others.

# Bibliography

Allen, Helena G., *The Betrayal of Liliuokalani—Last Queen of Hawaii.* The Arthur H. Clark Co., 1982

Allen, John, ed., *One Hundred Great Lives.* Greystone Press/Hawthorn Books, 1944

Anderson, Marian, *My Lord, What A Morning.* The Viking Press, 1956

Anger, Kenneth, *Hollywood Babylon.* Dell Publishing Co., Inc., 1975

Armstrong, Louis, *Satchmo—My Life in New Orleans.* Prentice–Hall, Inc., 1954

Arnold, Schwinn & Company, *Fifty Years of Schwinn–Built Bicycles.* Arnold, Schwinn & Company, 1945

Atkinson, Eleanor, *Johnny Appleseed—The Romance of the Sower.* Harper & Brothers, 1943

Bade, William Frederic, *The Life and Letters of John Muir.* Houghton Mifflin Company, 1924

Bailey, Paul, *Those Kings and Queens of Old Hawaii.* Westernlore Books, 1975

Baker, Jean–Claude & Chase, Chris, *Josephine—The Hungry Heart.* Random House, 1993

Baker, Josephine & Bouillon, Jo, *Josephine* (Translated from the French by Mariana Fitzpatrick).
    Harper & Row, 1977

Balliet, Whitney, *Such Sweet Thunder—Forty–Nine Pieces on Jazz.*
    The Bobbs–Merrill Company, Inc., 1966

Barrett, S.M., ed., *Geronimo's Story of His Life.* Duffield & Company, 1906

Behrens, June, *Juliette Low—Founder of the Girl Scouts of America.* Children's Press, 1988

Bentley, E.C., ed., *The Best of Damon Runyon—A Choice Selection Made by E.C. Bentley.*
    Triangle Books, 1940

Berlin, Edward A., *King of Ragtime—Scott Joplin and His Era.* Oxford University Press, 1994

Berstein, Burton, *Thurber—A Biography.* Dodd, Mead & Company, 1975

Blain, Virginia/Grundy, Isobel/Clements, Patricia, *The Feminist Companion to Literature in English.*
    Yale University Press, 1990

Bontemps, Arna, *Famous Negro Athletes.* Dodd, Mead, & Co., 1964

Botkin, B.A. & Harlow, Alvin F., eds., *A Treasury of Railroad Folklore.* Bonanza Books, 1953

Bowler, Peter, *The Superior Person's Book of Words.* David R. Godine, 1985

Bowman, John S., *Andrew Carnegie—Steel Tycoon.* Silver Burdett Press, 1989

Bradford, Sarah, *Harriet Tubman—The Moses of Her People.* Corinth Books, 1961

Brady, Cyrus Townshend, *The Sioux Indian Wars.* Indian Head Books, 1992

Brashler, William, *The Story of Negro League Baseball.* Ticknor & Fields, 1994

Breslin, Jimmy, *Damon Runyon—A Life.* Dell Publishing, 1991

Browning, D.C. (Compiled after John W. Cousins), *Everyman's Dictionary of Literary Biography,
    English and American.* J.M. Dent & Sons, Ltd., 1962

Bruns, Robert A., *Preacher—Billy Sunday & Big–Time American Evangelism.*
    W.W. Norton & Company, 1992

Bryan III, J., *The World's Greatest Showman—The Life of P.T. Barnum.* Landmark Books, 1956

Burnett, Avis, *Gertrude Stein.* Atheneum, 1972

Burns, Eugene, *The Last King of Paradise.* Pellegrini & Cudahy, 1952

Callender, James H., *Yesterdays on Brooklyn Heights.* The Dorland Press, 1927

Candee, Marjorie Dent, ed., *Current Biography—1954.* H.W. Wilson Co., 1954

Carnegie, Andrew, *The Gospel of Wealth.* The Belknap Press of Harvard University Press, 1962

Chambers, Peggy, *A Doctor Alone.* Abelard–Schuman, 1958

Christopher, Milbourne, *Houdini—A Pictorial Life.* Thomas Y. Crowell Co., 1976

Circus Historical Society, "The Bandwagon", March–April and May–June 1971

Clark, John, ed., *Illustrated Biographical Dictionary.* Crescent Books, 1994

Connell, Evan S., *Son of the Morning Star.* Promontory Press, 1984

Cook, Fred J., *P.T. Barnum.* Encyclopedia Britannica Press, 1962

Cooper, Ilene, *Susan B. Anthony.* Franklin Watts, 1984

Cowan, Geoffrey, *The People v. Clarence Darrow.* Times Books/Random House, 1993

Cray, Ed, *Levi's.* Houghton Mifflin Co., 1978

Cronin, Edmund David, *Black Moses, The Story of Marcus Garvey and the U.N.I.A..*
    University of Wisconsin Press, 1955

Custer, Elizabeth Bacon, *Tenting on the Plains, or General Custer in Kansas and Texas.*
    Charles L. Webster & Company, 1887

Darrow, Clarence, *The Story of My Life.* Charles Scribner's Sons, 1932

De Caux, Len, *The Living Spirit of the Wobblies.* International Publishers, 1978

De Castro, Adolphe, *Portrait of Ambrose Bierce.* The Century Co., 1929

deCoy, Robert H., *The Big Black Fire.* Holloway House Publishing Co., 1969

Dethloff, Henry C., ed., *Huey P. Long—Southern Demagogue or American Democrat?.*
    D.C. Heath & Co., 1967

Dillon, Richard, *Wells, Fargo Detective—The Biography of James B. Hume.*
    Coward–McCann, Inc., 1969

Dockstader, Frederick J., *Great North American Indians—Profiles in Life and Leadership.*
    Van Nostrand Reinhold Co., 1977

Douglas, William O., *Muir of the Mountains.* Sierra Club Books for Children, 1994

Downs, Robert B./Flanagan, John T./Scott, Harold W., *More Memorable Americans 1750–1950.*
    Libraries Unlimited, 1985

Dubofsky, Melvyn, *We Shall Be All—A History of the IWW.* Quadrangle Books, 1969

Duncan, Isadora, *My Life.* Boni & Liveright, Inc., 1927

Eastman, John, *Who Lived Where.* Facts on File Publications, 1983

Eaton, Jeanette, *Trumpeter's Tale.* William Morrow & Company, 1955

Edmiston, Susan & Cirino, Linda D., *Literary New York.* Houghton Mifflin Company, 1976

Eno, Susan, ed., *Junior Girl Scout Handbook.* Girl Scouts of the U.S.A., 1986

Epstein, Jerry, *Remembering Charlie.* Bloomsbury Publishing Ltd., 1988

Erwin, Richard E., *The Truth About Wyatt Earp.* The O.K. Press, 1992

Everson, William K., *A Pictorial History of the Western Film.* The Citadel Press, 1969

Ewen, David, ed., *Popular American Composers from Revolutionary Times to the Present.*
    H.H. Wilson Co., 1962,
    *Great Men of American Popular Song.* Prentice–Hall, Inc., 1970,
    *Composers of Yesterday.* H.H. Wilson Co., 1937

Faber, Doris, *Oh Lizzie!—The Life of Elizabeth Cady Stanton.* Pocket Books, 1974

Farmer, Frances, *Will There Really Be A Morning?.* Dell Publishing Co., 1972

Fatout, Paul, *Ambrose Bierce—The Devil's Lexicographer.* University of Oklahoma Press, 1951

Feather, Leonard, *The Encyclopedia of Jazz.* Horizon Press, 1955

Feldman, Anthony & Ford, Peter, *Scientists & Inventors.* Facts on File, 1979

Fleischer, Nat, *The Heavyweight Championship.* G.P. Putnam's Sons, 1961

Flexner, Stuart Berg, *I Hear America Talking.* Simon and Schuster, 1976

Fox, Philip Charles, & Parkinson, Tom, *The Circus in America.* Country Beautiful, 1969

Freedman, Russell, *Indian Chiefs.* Holiday House, 1987

Frewin, Leslie, *The Late Mrs. Dorothy Parker.* Macmillan Publishing, Inc., 1986

Frommer, Harvey, *Jackie Robinson.* Franklin Watts, 1984

Gammond, Peter, *Scott Joplin and the Ragtime Era.* St. Martin's Press, 1975

Gardner, Robert & Shortelle, Dennis, *The Forgotten Players—The Story of Black Baseball in America.*
    Walker and Company, 1993

Giddens, Gary, *Satchmo.* Doubleday, 1988

Gifford, Denis, *Chaplin.* Macmillan London Ltd., 1974.

Gilmore, Al–Tony, *Bad Nigger! The National Impact of Jack Johnson.* Kennikat Press, 1975

Goodchild, Peter, *J. Robert Oppenheimer—Shatterer of Worlds.* Houghton Mifflin Co., 1981

Gould, Jean, *Miss Emily.* Houghton Mifflin Co., 1946,
    *Young Mariner Melville.* Dodd, Mead, & Company, 1956

Graham, Hugh Davis, ed., *Huey Long.* Prentice–Hall, Inc., 1970

Grattan, C. Hartley, *Bitter Bierce—A Mystery of American Letters.* Doubleday, Doran & Co., Inc., 1929

Gregory, Horace, *The World of James McNeill Whistler.* Thomas Nelson & Sons, 1959

Grodinsky, Julius, *Jay Gould, His Business Career 1867–1892.* University of Pennsylvania Press, 1957

Guthrie, Woody, *Bound For Glory.* E.P. Dutton & Co., Inc., 1943
    *Pastures of Plenty—A Self–Portrait.* Dave Marsh & Harold Leventhal, eds.
    Harper Collins Publishers, 1990
    *Seeds of Man.* E.P. Dutton & Co., Inc., 1976

Hacker, Louis M., *The World of Andrew Carnegie.* J.B. Lippincott Company, 1968

Hamilton, Virginia, *Paul Robeson—The Life and Times of a Free Black Man.* Harper & Row, 1974

Hampton, Wayne, *Guerrilla Minstrels.* The University of Tennessee Press, 1986

Havighurst, Walter, *Annie Oakley of the Wild West.* Macmillan Company, 1954

Hillway, Tyrus, *Herman Melville.* Twayne Publishers, Inc., 1963

Hine, Darlene Clark, ed., *Black Women in America—An Historical Encyclopedia.*
    Carlson Publishing Co., 1993

Hobhouse, Janet, *Everybody Who Was Anybody—A Biography of Gertrude Stein.*
    G.P. Putnam's Sons, 1975

Hodge, Frederick Webb, *Handbook of American Indians North of Mexico.* Pagent Books, Inc., 1959

Holiday, Billie with Dufty, William F., *Lady Sings the Blues.* Lancer Books, Inc. 1965

Howard, Leon, *Herman Melville—A Biography.* University of California Press, 1951

Howard, John Tasker, *Stephen Foster—America's Troubadour.* Tudor Publishing Co., 1943

Hoyt, Edwin P., *The Goulds.* Weybright and Talley, 1969

Humphrey, Kathryn Long, *Satchel Paige.* Franklin Watts, 1988

Hungerford, Edward, *Wells Fargo—Advancing the American Frontier.* Random House, 1949

Hunt, Mabel Leigh, *Better Known As Johnny Appleseed.* J.B. Lippincott Company, 1950

Hurok, Sol, *Impresario.* Random House, 1946

Jakoubek, Robert, *Jack Johnson.* Chelsea House Publishers, 1990

James, Edward T., ed., *Notable American Women 1607–1950—A Biographical Dictionary.*
    The Belknap Press of the Harvard University Press, 1971

Jones, Max and Chilton, John, *Louis—The Louis Armstrong Story.* Little, Brown and Company, 1971

Judson, Clara Ingram, *Andrew Carnegie.* Follett Publishing Co., 1964

Kaplan, Justin, *Mr. Clemens and Mark Twain—A Biography.* Simon and Schuster, 1966

Keats, John, *You Might As Well Live—The Life and Times of Dorothy Parker.*
    Simon and Schuster, 1970

Keegan, John & Wheatcroft, Andrew, *Who's Who in Military History.*
    William Morrow & Co., Inc., 1976

Kellogg, Steven, *Johnny Appleseed.* Morrow Junior Books, 1988

Kelly, Emmett w/Kelly, F. Beverly, *Clown.* Prentice–Hall, Inc., 1954

Kingman, Russ, *A Pictorial Life of Jack London.* Crown Publishers, 1979

Kohn, George V., *Encyclopedia of American Scandal.* Facts on File, 1989

Kronenberger, Louis, ed., *Brief Lives.* Little, Brown and Company, 1971

Krythe, Maymie R., *All About American Holidays.* Harper & Brothers, 1962

Kudlinski, Kathleen V., *Juliette Gordon Low—America's First Girl Scout.* Viking Kestrel, 1988

Kugelmass, J. Alvin, *J. Robert Oppenheimer and the Atomic Story.* Julian Messner, Inc., 1953

Kunitz, Stanley J. & Haycraft, Howard, eds., *American Authors 1600–1900.*
H.W. Wilson and Company, 1938

Lake, Stuart N., *Wyatt Earp, Frontier Marshall.* Houghton Mifflin Co, 1931

Lancaster, Clay, *Old Brooklyn Heights.* Charles E. Tuttle Company, 1961

Laver, James, *Whistler.* Cosmopolitan Book Corporation, 1930

Levine, Issac Don, *Mitchell, Pioneer of Air Power.* Duell, Sloan and Pearce, 1943

Liliuokalani, Lydia, *Hawaii's Story by Hawaii's Queen.* Charles E. Tuttle Co., Inc., 1964

Lindsay, Vachel, *Johnny Appleseed and Other Poems.* The Macmillan Company, 1930

Logan, Rayford W. & Winston, Michael R., *Dictionary of American Negro Biography.*
W.W. Norton Co., 1982

Lomax, Alan/Guthrie, Woody/Seeger,Pete, *Hard Hitting Songs for Hard Hit People.*
Oak Publications, 1967

Loomis, Vincent V. w/Ethell, Jeffrey L., *Amelia Earhart—The Final Story.* Random House, 1985

Loveman, Samuel, *Twenty-One Letters of Ambrose Bierce.* George Kirk, 1922

Manchester, Harland, *Trail Blazers of Technology.* Charles Scribner's Sons, 1962

Martin, Thomas Commerford, *Inventions, Researches, and Writings of Nikola Tesla.*
Originally published in "The Electrical Engineer", 1894; modern edition: Angriff Press, 1981

Mast, Gerald, *The Comic Mind—Comedy and the Movies.* Bobbs-Merrill Co., 1973

Medearis, Angela Shelf, *Little Louis and the Jazz Band.* Lodestar Books, 1994

McCabe, John, *George M. Cohan: The Man Who Owned Broadway.* Doubleday & Co., Inc., 1973

McCaffrey, Donald W., ed., *Focus on Chaplin.* Prentice-Hall, Inc., 1971

McCarthy, Albert et. al., *Jazz on Record.* Hanover Books, 1968

McKissack, Patricia C. & McKissack Jr., Frederick, *Black Diamond—The Story of the Negro Baseball Leagues.* Scholastic, Inc., 1994

McLoughlin Jr., William G., *Billy Sunday Was His Real Name.* The University of Chicago Press, 1955

McPherson, Aimee Semple, *The Personal Testimony of Aimee Semple McPherson.*
Heritage Committee, 1966

Meade, Marion, *Dorothy Parker—What Fresh Hell Is This?.* Villard Books, 1988

Mellow, James R., *Charmed Circle—Gertrude Stein & Company.* Praeger Publishers, 1974

Metcalf, Eleanor Melville, *Herman Melville—Cycle and Epicycle.* Harvard University Press, 1953

Michelmore, Peter, *The Swift Years—The Robert Oppenheimer Story.* Dodd, Mead & Co., 1969

Miller, Lee O., *The Great Cowboy Stars of Movies and Television.* Arlington House Publishers, 1979

Mitchell, Ruth, *My Brother Bill.* Harcourt Brace & Co., 1953

Mix, Paul E., *The Life and Legend of Tom Mix.* A.S. Barnes & Company, 1972

Mooney, Booth, *General Billy Mitchell.* Follett Publishing Co., 1968

Moore, Virginia, *Distinguished Women Writers.* E.P. Dutton & Co., Inc., 1934

Morehouse, Ward, *George M. Cohan—Prince of the American Theatre.* J.P. Lippincott Co., 1943

Morsberger, Robert E., *James Thurber.* Twayne Publishers, 1964

Muir, John, *Letters to a Friend.* Houghton Mifflin Company, 1915

Nash, Jay Robert, *Encyclopedia of Western Lawmen and Outlaws.* Paragon House, 1992

Newman, Shirlee P., *Marian Anderson: Lady From Philadelphia.* The Westminster Press, 1966

Nisenson, Samuel & Parker, Alfred, *Minute Biographies.* Grosset & Dunlap, 1931

Noble, Iris, *Clarence Darrow—Defense Attorney.* Julian Messner, Inc., 1958

Norman, Charles, *John Muir, Father of Our National Parks.* Julian Messner, Inc., 1957

O'Connor, Richard, *Gould's Millions.* Doubleday & Company, Inc., 1962
*Sitting Bull, War Chief of the Sioux.* McGraw-Hill, 1968

O'Meally, Robert, *Lady Day—The Many Faces of Billie Holiday.* Arcade Publishing, 1991

O'Neil, John J., *Prodigal Genius—The Life of Nikola Tesla.* Ives Washburn, 1944

Pace, Mildred Mastin, *Juliette Low.* Charles Scribner's Sons, 1947

Paul, Elliot, *That Crazy American Music.* The Bobbs-Merrill Company, Inc., 1957

Pearce, John Ed, *The Colonel.* Doubleday & Co., Inc., 1982

Pearson, Hesketh, *The Man Whistler.* Harper & Brothers Publishers, 1952

Petry, Ann, *Harriet Tubman—Conductor on the Underground Railroad.* Thomas Y. Crowell Co., 1955

Pitts, Michael R., *Western Movies—A TV and Video Guide to 4200 Genre Films.*
McFarland & Co., Inc., 1986

Porter, David L., ed., *Biographical Dictionary of American Sports—Baseball.* Greenwood Press, 1987

Porter, Roy, consultant ed., *The Biographical Dictionary of Scientists (2nd Edition).*
Oxford University Press, 1994

Pukui, Mary Kawena, *Hawaiian Dictionary: Hawaiian–English, English–Hawaiian.*
University of Hawai'i Press, 1986

Rawling, Gerald, *The Pathfinders—The History of America's First Westerners.*
The Macmillan Company, 1964

Rennert, Richard, ed., *Jazz Stars.* Chelsea House Publishers, 1994

Roberts, Randy, *Papa Jack—Jack Johnson and the Era of White Hopes.* The Free Press, 1983

Rogers, W.G., *When This You See Remember Me: Gertrude Stein in Person.*
Rinehart & Company, 1948

Rose, Phyllis, *Jazz Cleopatra—Josephine Baker in Her Time.* Doubleday, 1989

Ross, Ishbel, *Child of Destiny.* Harper & Brothers, 1949

Saxon, A.H., *P.T. Barnum—The Legend and the Man.* Columbia University Press, 1989

Schoor, Gene w/Gilford, Henry, *The Jim Thorpe Story—America's Greatest Athlete.*
Julian Messner, 1969

Scott, Richard, *Jackie Robinson.* Chelsea House Publishers, 1987

Seeger, Pete, *The Incompleat Folksinger.* Simon & Schuster, 1972

Shatzkin, Mike, ed., *The Ballplayers.* Arbor House, William Morrow, 1990

Sherr, Lynn & Kazickas, Jurate, *Susan B. Anthony Slept Here—A Guide to American Women's Landmarks.* Times Books/Random House, 1994

Sicherman, Barbara and Green, Carol Hurd, *Notable American Women—The Modern Period.*
The Belknap Press of the Harvard University Press, 1980

Sifakis, Carl, *American Eccentrics.* Facts on File Publications, 1984

Smith, Alice Kimball & Weiner, Charles, eds., *Robert Oppenheimer—Letters and Recollections.*
Harvard University Press, 1980

Smith, Jesse Carney, ed., *Notable Black American Women.* Gale Research, Inc., 1992

Speaight, George, *The Book of Clowns.* Macmillan Publishing Co., 1980

Sprigge, Elizabeth, *Gertrude Stein—Her Life and Work.* Harper & Brothers, 1957

Stegner, Wallace, *The Preacher and the Slave.* Houghton Mifflin Company, 1950

Stewart–Gordon, John, *Saga of the "Chicken" Colonel.* Reader's Digest, 2/75
(from "Louisville Magazine", 1/75)

Stone, Irving, *Sailor on Horseback—The Biography of Jack London.* 1938

Tabrah, Ruth M., *Hawaii—A History.* W.W. Norton & Co., Inc., 1980

Tedards, Anne, *Marian Anderson.* Chelsea House Publishers, 1988

Thurber, James, *The Seal in the Bedroom and Other Predicaments.* Harper & Brothers, 1932
*The Thurber Carnival.* Harper & Row, 1945
*The Years With Ross.* Little, Brown and Company, 1959

Tompert, Ann, *The Greatest Showman on Earth.* Dillon Press, 1987

Totheroh, Dan, *Johnny Appleseed—A Play in Two Acts.* Bohemian Club, 1946

Truitt, Evelyn Mack, *Who Was Who On Screen.* R.R. Bowker Co., 1974

Twain, Mark, *The Adventures of Huckleberry Finn.* Samuel L. Clemens, 1884

Ulanov, Barry, *A History of Jazz in America.* The Viking Press, 1952

Van Steenwyk, Elizabeth, *Levi–Strauss—The Blue Jeans Man.* Walker & Co., 1988

Vernoff, Edward & Shore, Rima, *The International Dictionary of 20th Century Biography.*
New American Library, 1987

Walker, Franklin, *The Wickedest Man in San Francisco.* The Colt Press, 1941

Wallechinsky, David & Wallace, Irving, *The People's Almanac.* Doubleday & Co., 1975
*The People's Almanac #2.* Bantam Books, 1978

Waters, Frank, *The Earp Brothers of Tombstone.* Clarkson N. Potter, Inc., 1960

Weidhorn, Manfred, *Jackie Robinson.* Antheum, Macmillan Publishing Co., 1993

Weiner, Ed, *The Damon Runyon Story.* Longmans, Green, & Co., 1948

Weintraub, Stanley, *Whistler—A Biography.* Weybright and Talley, 1974

Weisberg, Barbara, *Susan B. Anthony—Woman Suffragist.* Chelsea House Publishers, 1988

Wheeler, Robert W., *Jim Thorpe—World's Greatest Athlete.* University of Oklahoma Press, 1979

Whitcomb, Ian, *After the Ball—Pop Music From Rag to Rock.* Simon and Schuster, 1972

Whitman, Alden, ed., *American Reformers.* The H.W. Wilson Co., 1985

Wiggins, Robert A., *Ambrose Bierce.* University of Minnesota Press, 1964

Williams, Beryl & Epstein, Samuel, *The Great Houdini—Magician Extraordinary.*
Julian Messner, 1950

Williams, Oscar, ed., *The Pocket Book of Modern Verse.* Pocket Books, 1974

Williams, T. Harry, *Huey Long.* Alfred A. Knopf, 1969

Wilson, Neill C., *Treasure Express—Epic Days of the Wells Fargo.* The Macmillan Company, 1938

Wiltsey, Norman B., *Brave Warriors.* The Caxton Printers, Ltd., 1963

Wisniewski, Richard A., *The Rise and Fall of the Hawaiian Kingdom.* Pacific Basin Enterprises, 1979

Yost, Nellie Snyder, *Buffalo Bill—His Family, Friends, Fame, Failures, and Fortunes.* SageBooks, 1979

Yurchenco, Henrietta, *Mighty Hard Road.* McGraw–Hill Book Company, 1970

*The Baseball Encyclopedia*—9th Edition. Macmillan Publishing Co., 1993

*The American Heritage Book of Great Adventures of the Old West*, American Heritage Press, 1969

*Dictionary of American Biography*, Charles Scribner's Sons, 1934

*Lincoln Library of Sports Champions*, Frontier Press Company, 1993

*National Cyclopedia of American Biography—Being the History of the United States*,
James T. White & Co., 1939; 1984

*The Negro Almanac—A Reference Work on the Afro–American* (4th Edition).
John Wiley & Sons, 1983

*Story of the Great American West*, Reader's Digest Association, 1977

*The Women*, 1978; *The Trailblazers*, 1973: Time–Life Books

*Webster's American Biographies*, G. & C. Merriam Co., 1975

*Webster's American Military Biographies*, G. & C. Merriam Co., 1978

*Who Was Who In America, Volume 1, 1897–1942*, Marquis Publications, 1943

*IWW Songs of the Workers (The Little Red Songbook)—34th Edition.*
Industrial Workers of the World, 1980

And because they were invaluable concerning my attempts to capture authentic qualities of archaic diction and phraseology I'd like also to list, in the order they sit on my shelf, these titles:

*The Synonym Finder*, Rodale Press, Inc., 1978 *Roget's Thesaurus of Words and Phrases*, Grosset & Dunlap, 1941 *Shorter Oxford English Dictionary* (2 volume), Oxford University Press, 1933 *Webster's New World Dictionary of the American Language*, The World Publishing Company, 1966 *Dictionary of Foreign Terms*, by C.O. Sylvester Mawson, Thomas Y. Crowell Company, 1934 *A Dictionary of Modern American Usage*, H.W. Fowler, Oxford University Press, 1944 *The New York Times Style Book for Writers and Editors*, McGraw–Hill Book Company, 1962 *Soule's Dictionary of English Synonyms*, Tudor Publishing Company, 1946 (1871) *Putnam's Word Book*, by Louis A. Flemming, G.P. Putnam's Sons, 1914 *American Dialect Dictionary*, by Harold Wentworth, Thomas Y. Crowell Company, 1944 *Funk & Wagnalls Standard Handbook of Synonyms, Antonyms, and Prepositions*, by James C. Fernald, Funk & Wagnalls Company, 1947 (1914) *Putnam's Phrase Book*, A.L. Burt Company, 1919 *Crabb's English Synonyms*, by George Crabb, Harper & Brothers, 1903 *The Roget Dictionary of Synonyms and Antonyms*, by C.O. Sylvester Mawson, G.P. Putnam's Sons, 1931 *The Dictionary of Americanisms*, by John Russell Bartlett, Crescent Books, 1989 (1849) *Roget's Thesaurus of the English Language in Dictionary Form*, by C.O. Sylvester Mawson, Garden City Publishing Company, Inc., 1931 *Webster's Dictionary of Synonyms*, G. & C. Merriam Co., Publishers, 1951 (1942) *1811 Dictionary of the Vulgar Tongue–A Dictionary of Buckish Slang, University Wit, and Pickpocket Eloquence*, Bibliophile Books, 1984 (1811)